THE GOOD PAGAN'S FAILURE

THE GOOD PAGAN'S FAILURE

BY

ROSALIND MURRAY

Sine tuo numine
Nihil est in homine

LONGMANS, GREEN AND CO.
NEW YORK ✧ TORONTO
1948

"You have heard and know that there are two cities, for the present mingled together in body, but in heart, separated. One, whose end is eternal peace, is called Jerusalem, the other, whose joy is temporal peace, is called Babylon."

—St. Augustine.

CONTENTS

I

CHRISTIAN AND PAGAN

"Unless the Lord build the house, they labour in vain that build it."

—Ps. cxxvi.

."Religion is the opium of the people."

"The freedom with which Christ has made us free."

How can these two descriptions apply to the same idea?
How is it possible for the same thing to appear in so diametrically opposed a light, to people of an identical civilization and
epoch, equally intelligent, equally good and sincere, formed
by the same social experience, the same cultural background,
in all external respects and with the same material facts upon
which to base their judgments?

It is bewildering to contemplate such a complete and absolute contradiction, yet we are all aware that it exists; most of
us take it for granted as one of the numerous differences of
opinion to which we grow accustomed as a part of the essential
texture of our life; yet if we pause to consider these two statements with a little more attention, we realize that this absolute
contradiction is more than a mere difference of opinion; each
professes, at least, to be a statement of fact, and these two
facts are incompatible.

It is possible for different people to hold entirely opposing
points of view about something with which both have come
in contact, a picture they both have seen, a book they both
have read, a person known to both, but in such cases we find
some large basis of fact agreed. There will be agreement as
to the size and colour of the picture, though one may pronounce it good, another, bad; there will be agreement as to
the length and subject of the book, though one judges it well

3

written, the other badly; the same holds good of our common acquaintance; we can recognize the same subject of discussion although we differ in our views about it; but in these two definitions of religion, there seems to be no common ground at all.

If we pursue our definition further we shall find the contradiction become only more explicit; are we in fact discussing the same subject, or are we talking at cross purposes?

"Religion is the opium of the people." We are all familiar with that point of view, it extends far beyond the ranks of loyal Marxists, it is the generally accepted orthodoxy among "enlightened" intellectuals.

Those among us who have grown up in such circles will have imbibed it from our infancy, without bitterness or fanatical abhorrence, but as a platitude, a *chose jugée*; we can see that the "thing judged" was a bad thing, but was this "thing," in actual fact, religion?

The present writer remembers well, as a child, hearing slighting references to an "Old Man" in the sky sending people to Hell, which were rightly calculated to rule out such religion as a possible point of view for decent people; the sense of the ludicrous and incongruous in the attributes and behaviour of the Old Man was allied with deeper and more dangerous moral feelings; how could an intelligent rational being accept a morality based upon such barbarism? The answer was, of course, that he could not, but neither question nor answer took one further. The bogey set up like a coco-nut to be shied at was duly pelted and knocked down, but what significance had such a bogey? The blows at him were not blows at religion.

We have examples of this presentation in such books as Mr. Shaw's *Black Girl in Search of God*. Militant atheists are often moral men; they are truly attacking something evil. The word "religion" stands, in their imagination, for Torquemada as they picture him, or perhaps the monkey trial in Tennessee; they see a weight of cruelty and evil throughout the history of humanity, a stifling of everything they know as good, connected with or attributed to religion. "*Tantum religio potuit suadere malorum*" is for them the battle-cry to which they rally. The religious man may reply in the same language: "*Corruptio optimi pessima.*"

You have not in fact dealt with your opponent if it is his caricature, and that only, that you deal with. To take examples of religious corruption as religion is to make an elementary mistake.

There have been and there are depraved agnostics; what outrages, what crimes are not committed, wrongly, in the name of human freedom? yet should we judge the true "enlightenment" by the debauches of red fanatics? With whatever point of view, with whatever faith we are dealing, we must consider it in its essential form, in its "idea," not travestied and perverted and destroyed.

Yet by doing justice to our adversary we do not liquidate our differences; it is not only hostile misrepresentation that faces us; that can be cleared away by goodwill and love of truth, but we find, when we carry our inquiry further, that the contradictory evidence increases; we cannot see this thing in the same light.

From the standpoint of the enlightened rationalist, religion stands for illusion and limitation, a refusal to face the truth, a shirking of natural responsibility, a narrowing and foreshortening of horizon, a deliberate attempt to escape reality.

Now there would be general agreement, from both sides, that the tendencies thus described were to be deplored, that

they were, in current terms, "anti-social," "regressive,"
"disintegrating," "non-adult," or, in the older terminology,
that they were "bad," but here agreement ends, for we find
that it is precisely these same failings that the religious man
ascribes to "rationalism."

The believer does not say: "These things are unimportant;
I may be, as you say, limited, afraid of truth or responsibility,
I may be taking refuge in illusion, but it does not matter,
because you are so much worse in other ways." He takes the
war into the enemy's country, he joins issue upon the same
contention; his line of argument is more as follows:

"The weaknesses that you ascribe to me are forms of
natural common human weakness; as man, I am undoubtedly
subject to all the tendencies with which you charge me, but,"
he would say, "in so far as I am a Christian, I have been
liberated from their domination; the horizon of my life has
been extended beyond the limits of my human fear. I do not
fear the truth, I apprehend it. In so far as the faith I affirm is
real to me, I share the freedom of the Sons of God."

To him the rationalist builds on an illusion, to him he
escapes from hard reality into an imagined world of perfect
or perfectable human beings; to him the boundless world of
time and space, of eternity and infinity and God, has been
limited and confined intolerably, by rationalism, into the tiny
world of here and now. He cannot breathe or move in such
constriction, shut off from all the outer air and light.

We find the same contradiction in outlook spreading outward through all the ramifications of ideas, affecting all our
secondary judgments; there is a logic, an interdependence in
our ideas of which we are often only half aware. Our judgments, our moral principles, our beliefs are not, as is so commonly assumed, disjointed separate arbitrary decisions, inde-

pendent of any central root; they are in fact inextricably woven into, inter-related with, contingent on, our basic and essential principle.

The attitude with which we face the world, the elemental fact from which we start, must determine to a very large extent our subsequent reactions and position towards the different aspects of our life.

The contemporary world is atomic in its outlook; dissociated ideas, emotions, sense impressions, are almost deliberately cultivated at the expense of continuous or long-distance considerations; cause and effect, dependence and relation are at a discount, and to the atomic mind the realization of such underlying unity is alien and distasteful.

In attempting to explain to ourselves and to each other the differences of which we are both aware, we find that we are handicapped at the outset by lack of common ground from which to start, a common language in which to speak; and yet we want to communicate with each other. It seems at times as though we were divided by a deep narrow chasm across which there is no bridge, by a thick veil through which we partly see, but through which we can never touch each other. That we should not be so separate and divided, we both in varying degrees agree, yet how to meet we neither of us know.

To a great many of our contemporaries, religious difference itself appears of no importance. The question of our ultimate belief in God, in any supernatural life, is secondary, irrelevant to the conduct of this life, yet they too would be conscious of divisions in what to them are more important questions: "Left" and "Right" opinions in politics, progressive or reactionary principles, congenial or uncongenial social outlook.

Religious belief, as such, will play so small a part in the conscious content of their minds that they will not know how far, in this respect, they agree with, or differ from, their acquaintance—in many cases, with or from their friends. The conscious ground of difference may be shifted from the immaterial to the material medium, but we have not, by so doing, overcome it; we may shirk the primal and essential issue, at least temporarily, in this way, but its secondary implications and consequences present themselves to us at every turn.

We do not suggest that existing political parties, or any political parties at any time, represent or replace religious standpoints, nor yet that political or social readjustment could compensate for the fundamental differences; what we do suggest is that, under present conditions, religious difference and conflict has been temporarily succeeded and obliterated by more temporal and material forms of conflict, that the interest and emotion which formerly were projected into religious controversy, at times with tragic consequences, are to-day transferred into the material field, but that this diversion of interest is in its nature only symptomatic of a more general movement in the same direction, the deliberate transference of all interest and all value from "other-worldly" value to "this-worldly," which has been taking place throughout Western Europe for at least the last four centuries of our era. Where our treasure is, there too will be our conflict. It is our contention that the essential difference which separates and divides us human beings, is still, and always must be, spiritual, in whatever material guise it is presented, and that, whether we recognize it or ignore it, all more immediate obvious difference is ultimately dependent upon one, acceptance or rejection of belief in God, in the full sense and meaning that this implies.

It is our contention that the difference implied in our different attitudes to God is fundamental through all forms of our life, that our attitude on this ultimate, fundamental question determines the whole direction of our living in all its aspects and in all relations, and that opposition in this one decisive matter implies secondary, but resultant, opposition in outlook and in value throughout our lives. The following pages are a rough attempt to define and understand this opposition, to let us recognize our own positions more clearly and distinctly than we do. It is not suggested that differences will vanish, that through understanding we shall agree; on the contrary, I believe that, in some cases, a clearer realization of the position will deepen and intensify the cleavage which does divide the opposing points of view, but it is our belief that such an inquiry will alter the perspective of our approach; we shall gain at least some comprehension of the nature of our divisions, and that in itself must be a step in the right direction. We must know the true character of our adversary before we can either conquer or persuade him.

In any consideration of this nature, it is impossible to be quite impartial. If we have thought about such things at all, we have inevitably come to some conclusions; if once we have recognized the supreme importance of the issue now before us and its vital effect upon our actual lives, it becomes impossible to remain neutral, detached spectators of the conflict. We are bound to range ourselves on one side or the other. We must know our own position and defend it, yet, if our discussion is to serve any purpose, we must endeavour to state the issue fairly; we must try, so far as we are able, to see ourselves as our opponents see us, to regard the question from their point of view.

Here it seems necessary, for a moment, to write more personally; the task we have set before us is ambitious, and I approach it most acutely conscious of limitations and inadequacy; one qualification, and one only, I possess—actual experience of both points of view.

Born and brought up among enlightened Pagans, their outlook, and their standards and their values, are those which I first knew, by which I was educated; the Pagan world of limited perfection was that familiar to me, as I grew up.

In maturity I have found enlightened Paganism inadequate to explain life as I see it, inadequate to deal with it as I find it. The picture presented to me in youth has proved, so it seems to me, a misleading picture, the account of existence offered, a false account; the key with which I was furnished, unlocks no door.

I have found that the Christian world-picture, world-story, explanation, does fit the world that I know and have to live in; the alternative key, has, for me, unlocked the door.

With no reservation, no hesitation at all in this transferred allegiance, I retain a deep regard, a very real respect for the good Pagans whom I must now oppose. I must oppose, but I will not traduce them.

Having thus known both parties to the conflict, being accustomed to both languages, I am able, even now, to some extent, to see each side from the other's point of view.

It is my endeavour in the following pages to serve, in some measure, as an interpreter.

II

We have started from the position, which will be challenged, that a difference in fundamental religious outlook affects and influences our behaviour in almost every aspect of our life, that, in lines of thought and action far removed from the apparently religious field, this primal difference will assert

itself, that, however willing we may be, or think ourselves, to
sink our differences and co-operate across this immaterial
barrier, we cannot escape the consequent divisions, misunderstanding and antagonism.

If we agree upon existing evils, as to a large extent we find
we do, the agreement is only momentary; so soon as we attempt
to diagnose the sickness from which we find ourselves and our
society to be suffering, we meet the same absolute contradiction
in our ideas. There is, for example, very general agreement
that the contemporary post-war world is Pagan in every sense
in which the word is used; it is admitted readily from every
side and with *empressement*, as part of what we all deplore
about it; all the things we most dislike we label so. Fascism
and Communism in all their forms proclaim themselves as
Pagan openly, and nobody is likely to gainsay them, but
divergence comes when we begin to trace more deeply the
origin and the causes of these things. When we compare the
condemned autocracies with the old-established, approved,
democratic regimes, are we in logic to define these as Christian?
Ourselves, and France, and the United States? Or if we travel
back in time rather than in space, was our pre-war European
society really Christian? On the assumption that our culture
and background have been until now Christian, it has seemed
natural and reasonable to attribute our present evils to the
failure of Christianity, its inadequacy in facing modern problems, its inability to expand and modify and progress to suit
modern needs.

From one side it is stated as self-evident that Christianity
has been tried and has failed, that its day as an effective force is
over, that the present desperate state of civilization is conclu-
sive proof, were it required, of the absolute bankruptcy of
Christian values, the need for a remedy that is completely new.

On the other side, with equal certainty, the Christian will point to our present chaos as the most complete illustration of his thesis, as the natural and inevitable outcome of a Pagan domination of centuries. He will say without a shadow of hesitation that the Christian way of life has not yet been fully tried, that even through the centuries of Faith it has always been at grips with Paganism, at some periods more successfully, at others, less. He would claim that the Christian *Weltanschauung* did form and dominate our civilization at crucial periods of our history, he would assert its influence to be great through every century of Christian time, but that its hold had never been complete; the Pagan, he would say, was always latent in both individual and community. He would repeat that, not only in societies but in individuals, the conflict between the two views of life persists, that pure Christian and pure Pagan are both rare, that as in individuals and societies, so in ages, we shall, if we look, always find both tendencies, only in very different proportions; he would maintain that the difference in proportion does in fact amount to a difference in kind, and he would point to the centuries of our modern European civilization as supreme examples of such a conflict, in which, in ever-increasing proportion, the Christian values had been superseded by Pagan values. He would say that before the War, and long before it, the Pagan view of life was in the ascendant, that increasingly, in every generation, more of the Christian values had been discarded, the Pagan values more consciously acknowledged. He would in fact point to the present state of the world, our present troubles, as the quite foreseeable result of long progressive de-Christianization.

Here, I think, we should deal with a possible misconception: it is no part of our case that failure here and now is in itself a proof of error; by our whole contention of Pagan dominance we have admitted, at least temporarily, a failure of the half-established Christian culture; on a short view, we believe right often fails. The force of evil, of unregenerate, unredeemed human nature, does often, for a time, reject salvation; it is only on a Pagan assumption of human perfectibility that it should not. Does not the crucifixion of Our Lord, in itself, refute such judgment for a Christian? Our case is not that because the good Pagan civilization has now failed it is therefore rightly finished, but rather that, in the whole manner of its failing, the falsity of its elements are revealed. We say that, taking the empirical position, upon the basis of our Christian values (supposing them for the moment to be true), the present development and downfall of Pagan culture is what we should have predicted must happen, sooner or later.

What has happened is quite in accordance with expectation from our point of view, but not from the good Pagan's; on our calculation, the sum has worked out correctly; on his, the result is bewildering and unlooked for. It is noticeable that at the present time, when to most of the enlightened governing class in Europe the values and standards on which their life depended are dissolving and vanishing beneath their feet, the believing Christian is less disconcerted; he is less shocked at the manifestations of barbarism; in a sense, he is even less indignant and astonished at the re-emergence of militant atheism. It is the Good Pagan, the Humanist, the Liberal, who is completely aghast and outraged; what he sees and hears will not fit into his picture; he has no explanation and no comfort.

It may seem at first paradoxical and absurd to attribute to him the present devastation of his whole world, the downfall and overthrow of his own civilization, yet this is what we are setting out to do. We agree that he himself is the chief victim; we agree that in the rise of barbarism, which we are witnessing on every side, it is the Good Pagan who suffers the most acutely, who is the most completely overcome, to whom the ignoble and the barbarous are most excruciating and incomprehensible; indeed, he is apt to find fault with the Christian from a new angle, for being too tolerant, for not minding enough, not showing more indignation.

In truth, of course, the Christian dislikes no less than the Good Pagan the manifestations of this barbarism, but what he experiences is not new to him, he does not suffer from shock, as does the Pagan; he realizes, of course, that what is happening is worse and far more extreme than what he is used to, but in essence he sees it all as the same process working itself out to its own refutation. He has grown up, *qua* Christian, in a strange world of alien standards and values and behaviour; he is accustomed to being in disagreement with the world order in which he has to live; it is worse now than before, but not in its essence different.

To the Good Pagan, the gulf between Culture and Barbarism is the extreme and insuperable division; confronted with the present crude barbarism, he finds himself inclined towards the Christian: "Compared with these outsiders, we are one," is his reaction to the situation.

We know that family likeness is most noticeable to those outside the family; from inside, the various members seem quite unlike; so it is with the Good Pagan and the Barbarian. To themselves, they seem to stand at opposite poles, to the Christian, both are alike in non-belief. .

We seem to be faced with a deadlock in our inquiry; if we cannot agree as to our own condition, how can we hope to treat it? If we cannot agree as to what we are, what hope of

agreement as to what we ought to be? Are we perhaps misled
by our definitions? Do we really know what we mean by the
words "Christian" or "Christian civilization"? What is the
true opposing point of view?

We may agree that there are two distinct and conflicting
views of life, two essentially antagonistic scales of value, on
which to base our picture of the world, in which, by which to
live, and also die, but how to define these two opposing
pictures, how to recognize them, and assess them truly—this is
a great deal more difficult to do.

III

When we deplore the passing of an old order, when we say
that our culture is perishing or has perished, we imply that
what we are losing is of value, that what is going is better
than what has come, and this is very generally felt to-day. We
have seen that there is definite disagreement as to the character
of that culture, as to the cause and reason of its passing, but
whether we style it "Christian" or "Good Pagan," whether we
attribute its downfall to its own inherent weakness or to some
exterior, unforeseen disaster, there is a surprising measure of
agreement now, in its failure, that it was valuable, that we
regret it.

I believe that this sense of regret, of remorse almost, which
is so very generally felt, has contributed towards misunderstanding. We have grown so accustomed to consider ourselves
Christian, and our civilization to be in essence Christian, that
in current use the term has become synonymous with
"civilized."

The appropriation of the "Christian Ethic" by the Rationalist is but a part of a much wider process with which we must

deal later, in our consideration of the "Good Pagan"; it is, and has been, quite compatible with the rejection of religious value. According to such a standpoint, the "religious" have wrongly appropriated Christianity, and have perverted what was good moral teaching into a fantastic supernaturalism. According to this theory, the Gospels should be used with discrimination; such parts as are compatible with the rationalistic dogma may be retained, the rest is discarded as "extraneous." Seen in this light, St. John's Gospel and St. Paul are very much to blame for having distorted the Christian message; before their unwarranted interpolations we had an edifying and unobjectionable description of a great man, a great social reformer, with whom there need have been no difficulties. The "Christian Ethic," detached from its accretions, can be accepted to a large degree by the enlightened rationalistic mind.

From such a point of view, our civilization can be interpreted as a progressively enlightened development of this "Christian Ethic." If the essential point of Christianity is to be found in equalitarian social reform, it can be claimed that, to a quite considerable degree, such principles have in fact been operative increasingly through the last centuries. But is it, in fact, just this that we are losing?

On the contrary, I think it can be maintained that, in all the present confusion of moral value, the rejection and repudiation of accepted standards, this has alone survived; the emphasis on material well being, on social reform, as the sole criterion of progress, is only more dominant now and more exclusive. We find it predominant in the new social systems in Russia, in Germany, and in Italy, and in the most advanced circles in France and England it is equally recognized as of supreme importance.

It is not any less insistence on material progress that differentiates our contemporary society from its immediate, pre-War predecessor, that insistence they have in common, what is different is the present complete rejection of every other value of any kind, the denial of all the immaterial "quality" to which our pre-War culture still attached importance; the last vestige of non-material value has now gone.

If, then, true Christianity consists in social action in the material world, it could be urged that that, in fact, continues. From such a point of view, it might be said that *if* our pre-War modern society was Christian, so is the present.[1]

We are very much at the mercy of our words, and the meaning of words in current use changes, often imperceptibly, as we use them. The exact and definite meaning is blurred and distorted by careless use, sometimes accidentally, sometimes, and perhaps more often, from a half-conscious wish to modify it.

Both "Christian" and "Pagan" are words that have suffered thus. "Christian" is used to express vague approbation, sometimes implying general kindliness and tolerance, especially in relation to moral judgment, sometimes as meaning simply "civilized." These uses of the word are in themselves quite different, but both of them obscure and confuse its essential meaning. The same is largely true of the word "Pagan," it is thought of as complementary to "Christian"; if "Christian" is used in general approval, then "Pagan" expresses equivalent disapproval; if "Christian" is "civilized," "Pagan" is "uncivilized," if Christian" implies "kind," then "Pagan" implies "unkind."

The original careless use of the word Christian thus involves us in complementary difficulties, and the secondary miscon-

[1] Even the Nazi "Practical Christianity" would stand this test.

ception is more complete and flagrant than the first. Being "kind" and "civilized" is quite consistent with being Christian, although it is our contention that neither attribute is, in itself, at all an adequate equivalent, but to equate Pagan with cruel or uncivilized is an almost complete reversal of the truth.

The typical "Good Pagan" we are considering, on whom we declare our modern civilization to depend, is perhaps the most completely civilized being and also the most humane the world has known. An extreme sensitiveness to all forms of suffering, an extreme reluctance to pronounce moral judgment, are some of the signs by which we recognize him. He is the most polite, the most controlled, the most agreeable, of human beings, judged on the purely natural scale of values; he is the most perfected "natural man"; and because all the energies and potentialities of his nature are concentrated on his temporal culture, that culture too has developed to perfection, or at least to a large measure of perfection.

His values being all "relation-to-man" values, he is at his best in purely human relations, and so long as we do not endeavour to force him beyond the bounds of his own self-limitation, or to speak to him in a language he does not know; if we do that, we are pulled up abruptly, he cannot function outside his chosen medium, he cannot breathe another atmosphere; but there, on his own ground, he is supreme.

It is our purpose, so far as we are able, to use both words far more objectively, to describe two alternative, definite, points of view, two ways of life, to define by each a positive *Weltanschauung* which affects the society that it informs, and, so far as is compatible with our thesis, to use the terms without a moral bias.

It is inevitable that our personal standpoint should affect our judgment to some extent; we deceive ourselves if we deny it, but we must try to be as nearly impartial as is consistent with our own belief; with this in mind, we must first eliminate the more usual misconceptions that will meet us.

There is, as we have seen, a tendency to belittle our opponent, to misrepresent him, to facilitate our own victory by illusion, by too easy conquest of his substitute. This leads us nowhere and achieves no end. If we are seeking truth, how shall we find it by falsifying the problem we have to face?

We have seen that the materialist's conception of religion was misleading, that his attack was, in consequence, misdirected; if we in our turn are opposing Paganism, let us make sure that we do not travesty it. If Pagans were in fact uncivilized or cruel, if they were simply "bad," and Christians "good," the position would be quite other than it is.

In order to judge the two positions fairly, we must take the best examples from each side. The good Pagan will be better than the bad Christian; we believe the good Christian to be better still.

The use of the term Pagan in disparagement might seem at first to prove his own contention that European civilization has been Christian up till now. It is our answer that this use of words is in this case, as often, a relic from a previous scale of values. What is described as Pagan we disapprove of, that is true, but what is thus wrongly described is not Pagan. The phrase "Pagan worship of power," or "Pagan love of pomp," or of wealth, are examples, for although it is not Christian to prize such things, it is not necessarily Pagan either; the bad Christian and the bad Pagan succumb to such temptations, the good Christian and the good Pagan do not. Diogenes lived in a tub and eschewed the pleasures and amenities of life with a rigour that rivals St. Antony or St. Simeon; Marcus Aurelius endured the pomp and magnificence of empire with as little spiritual damage as St. Louis; Socrates gave his life for his faith as completely as did St. Lawrence, yet they were Pagans.

It is important that we should free ourselves from all suggestions of depreciation, yet equally we must keep clearly in our minds the reality and importance of our difference, the existence, when all misconceptions are removed, of an active and positive non-Christian moral standpoint; we will then see how far such a standpoint corresponds to the civilization we know, how far the standards and values we recognize as operative in our pre-war European culture correspond to those which actuate the non-Christian.

If we discard for the moment, as misleading, both terms we have been using, Christian and Pagan, perhaps it may help us to see more clearly the essential difference we are trying to define.

Deprived of labels, we may see the contrast as an emphasis on other-worldly value as opposed to this-worldly, on eternal as against temporal, on supernatural as against natural, on spiritual as against material, or, including and summing up all alternatives, recognition of God as the ultimate reality of life, or Man; this we maintain to be the essential difference, underlying and dominating all secondary divisions, not to be slurred over or explained away or ignored. We do not suggest that it is impossible to serve both God and Man; to serve our fellow men may be, and often is, an excellent form of service to Our Maker; but the end we have in view is all-important, and the relation in which we see our service. There cannot, in the very nature of things, be equal balance between Man and God, to imagine such equality is in itself denial of the whole idea of God.

"He who loves any other thing with God, makes light of Him, because he puts into the balance with Him that which is infinitely beneath Him. . . . There is nothing in the whole world to be compared with God, and therefore he who loves any other thing together with Him, wrongs Him. And if this be true, what does he do, who loves anything more than God?"[1]

The "difference" of God is no new idea; it has been fundamental from the beginning in the religious attitude to life, but it is as persistently ignored or contradicted in all the varying forms of non-belief. The old assertion that there is no God is less common in the contemporary world than the almost as misleading compromise of proposing this or that as "God-substitutes": service to Man, to the State, to Science, to abstract Knowledge, are offered to us as equivalent to God.

If we look at our pre-War culture from this angle, we may see it as an attempted mixture of these two quite contradictory points of view, belief in God as God, and at the same time, a still stronger belief in alternative God-substitutes.

According to the Christian *Weltanschauung*, such an attempt was by its nature foredoomed to failure, because it rested on a false assumption, a complete misconception of the nature of God, and consequent misconception of human nature.

We would repeat that in the admixture, the compromise, between the two contraries, the Pagan, material, temporal, point of view, had been increasingly predominant since what we think of as our "modern culture" asserted itself and broke loose from its medieval framework. We would say that the Christian standards and values had long since ceased to determine or control the general development of society; we would say that what we look back to now as passing, the era of enlightened liberalism, of a cultivated, oligarchic domination,

[1] St. John of the Cross. *Ascent of Mount Carmel*, Bk. I, v. 4.

was in its essential character Pagan, but Paganism of an exalted type, and that what we are experiencing to-day is but a further stage in the same process of ever-increasing materialization.

IV

Mr. Christopher Dawson has ably shown, in his *Making of Europe*, how the impact of Christian culture on the Barbarian produced our Western European civilization; he has shown how the countries north of the Rhine revolted, how the Nordic races were never quite civilized, never completely part of the civilized Christian world; I would like to carry this theory further; I doubt if the Latin races were ever quite Christian either. The impact, in their case, was of another kind, it was Christianity against the cultured Pagan, the sophisticated, disillusioned gentleman, instead of the barbarous and un-tutored savage, but the fusion was not complete in either case; it modified and controlled and sublimated, it created and guided European culture, but the Pagan was still there in both his forms, underneath the dominant culture he accepted, ready to break out in revolt and self-assertion when the strain upon him should become too acute, when the guiding spirit faltered or was weakened.

In France, he revolted in the eighteenth century, in Germany with the Aufklärung, and again, in a second burst, with the rise of Prussia, no need to wait for Herr Baldur von Schirach to proclaim it; in Italy he broke loose in the Renaissance, again with new vigour at the Risorgimento, and he is ascendant now and vocal and unashamed; in England, as long ago as the Tudors, the essential paganism of the governing class asserted itself deliberately, and prevailed.

The question as to how far, and how deeply, Europe was

ever Christian, is a difficult one to answer. In any age we shall find the great mass of public opinion undecided, indefinite, ready to take its colour and direction from a positive and determined minority. If we take as our "type" the Totalitarian Christian, the saint, to whom God and supernatural value are of supreme importance, whose whole life and interest centre upon God, it is obvious that there has never been a time when all, or even a majority, have been such Christians; the totalitarian Christian has been, always, rare, but one saint may sanctify his generation, and it is equally true that there have been periods, and long periods, when Christian sanctity did dominate men's minds, at least as an ideal, when the other-worldly Christian values were generally accepted as valid by the great mass of indeterminate public opinion, in the same way as opposing Pagan values are generally and unthinkingly accepted at the present day. Such epochs we may designate as Christian.

As examples of the contrast in public opinion, we may compare the figures round whom mass enthusiasm collects at different times. We can read the account of St. Bernard of Clairvaux's journeys through Italy, and again through Germany, in the twelfth century, how the crowds streamed out to meet him from the cities whose bells were pealing news of his approach, how he was surrounded, pressed upon, almost crushed by the excited devotion of the masses. "One day at Frankfort he was saved from imminent death when the Emperor Conrad, lifting his frail body babywise, carried him over the heads of the crowd amid a delirious din in which saint-worship, admiration for a brawny sovereign, and pity, had each their part."[1] We are struck by the contrast to the present day.

[1] *A Cloistered Company* by H. C. Mann.

The only comparable scenes in modern times are those which greet the arrival of some film star. When Mary Pickford visited this country a few years back, the scenes evoked by her appearance rivalled these; on more than one occasion, at least, the police were obliged to play the part of the Emperor Conrad, to protect her forcibly from her admirers.

The World's Little Sweetheart, as against St. Bernard . . . if we consider these contrasted figures, it seems superfluous to continue further, yet I believe that, to many modern readers, this actual example may lack cogency from absence of any impression of St. Bernard. They will know the dogs and the Pass, perhaps the Hospice, nothing further.[1] Let us then emphasize St. Bernard as an example of an austere and uncompromising devotion, no pleasant, easily sentimentalized type of saint, essentially totalitarian in his outlook, representing a totalitarian expectation.

We may also point out, incidentally, for the benefit of Left-Wing internationalists, that he was a Frenchman, and that the reception which we have recorded took place in Germany; there were similar scenes when he travelled in Italy; can we imagine to-day that any Frenchman, representative and acclaimed in his own country, would receive equivalent popular recognition in what we think of as the "opposing" countries?

The recognition accorded to St. Bernard, a Frenchman, by the populace in both Germany and Italy sums up in one example many aspects of the contracted values of our world. His nationality was of no account, nor was his class (he was the son of noble parents); these barriers of to-day were unimportant; he was their saint, their ideal, their possession; because of him, they too were sanctified. They did not feel resentful or

---

[1] Although even these belong to another St. Bernard.

envious of him, they did not feel cut off and separate, at a
disadvantage, or belittled through his merit. They shared his
world, his values, they belonged, in minor places, to his
hierarchy. We have thus, in this example, an illustration of
what is implied in Christian unity, the totalitarian, hierarchic
order, the relation of parts to whole, in supernatural value, as
opposed to the atomic, equalitarian standpoint, the struggle for
life, the free competition, of our Good Pagan democratic
order.

There are very many similar examples to be cited from lives
of saints in other centuries, both earlier and later than St.
Bernard.

To give exact dates at which the general outlook, thus
illustrated, changed, would not be easy. It is an essential part
of our contention that the two points of view, the two conflicting values, are always present, in differing proportions, in all
ages.

We can safely assert, however, that, in the main, this
other-worldly, totalitarian state of mind prevailed, as an ideal,
from some time in the third century A.D. until some time in the
fifteenth century, in varying degrees in the various parts of
Europe, and that its decline, or rather its supersession, by the
more material Pagan valuation, has been a steady and continuous process, ever since that period to the present day;
more recently, in the post-War era, the rate of change has
been accelerated.[1]

[1] That this fact is recognized by an authority in whose judgment the
value of the process is reversed is shown in the following passage from
Sir James Frazer's *Golden Bough* (published 1914), pp. 299–301.
"The saint and the recluse disdainful of Earth and wrapt in ecstatic
contemplation of Heaven, became in popular opinion the highest ideal
of Humanity. The earthly city seemed poor and contemptible to men
whose eyes beheld the City of God coming in the clouds of Heaven. . . .
This obsession lasted for a thousand years. The revival of Roman Law,

V

In the foregoing pages we have suggested that the present
disastrous condition of civilization is due to the failure of
Good Pagan, not Christian, culture. We have admitted that
Europe was once Christian predominantly, though never yet
completely. We do not admit that the Christian culture has
been tried and found inadequate, we maintain, on the contrary,
that it has not as yet been fully tried; we assert, moreover,
that, during the centuries in which its influence was most
dominant, in which the Christian value and world order was
most generally and profoundly recognized, civilization was, in
fundamental respects, better, values were truer, the principles
upon which human life was based, at least ideally, were
sounder; we have given, as illustrations of the change in fundamental ideal, St. Bernard of Clairvaux and Mary Pickford, as
centres of popular enthusiasm. It is our contention that in later
ages of our civilization we have experienced, to a large degree,
not progress, as was popularly supposed, but regression; that
the line of development which society has followed, upon
which our culture and our minds have been formed, is not, as
has been supposed, a progressive development of the Christian
outlook, a re-interpretation and re-adaptation of Christian
truth, but rather a rebellion against that order, a repudiation
and rejection of that truth.

We have admitted that it is difficult to assign an exact date
for such a revaluation, but we may accept, as roughly justified,

---

of the Aristotelian philosophy, of Ancient Art and Literature, at the
close of the Middle Ages marked the return of Europe to native ideals of
life and conduct, to saner, manlier views of the world. The long halt of
civilization was over. The tide of Oriental invasion had turned at last.
It is ebbing still."

the usual dating of our modern European civilization from some time in the fifteenth or sixteenth century, the time of the Renaissance and the Reformation.

We should agree with the usual assertion that these centuries marked a decisive turning-point in our civilization, that that time, like our own, was a time of transition and upheaval, a repudiation of accepted standards, a clearing of the ground for some new thing, but in our view what emerged then was not in fact new at all, it was the old paganism of the Ancient World, breaking loose from the framework of Christian civilization, by which it had been confined and controlled and changed.

We suppose it new because, however we name it, it is felt to be, as it is, the basis of modern Europe; but it may be modern, without being new.

On this supposition, which we shall try to prove, what is happening now, in the world round about us, is but a further stage in that revolt; the first, back from Christian culture to Pagan culture; now back from Pagan culture to barbarism: in time, seen as two stages in development, in value, as two stages in regression.

In treating our civilization as Pagan, it is important that we should recognize the internal quality of such paganism; it is in itself a highly developed culture, imposed on undifferentiated barbarism. We have referred to the two kinds of paganism on which the Christian culture was imposed, the Northern Barbarian, and the sophisticated Latin, but we must realize that these two forms of paganism were, in themselves, at totally different levels. The Latin humanistic paganism was, and had been for centuries, a dominant, highly developed, specialized culture, in which such Barbarian elements were subdued.

If we say that throughout twelve centuries the Christian culture dominated both, but that the Pagan beneath was never permeated, we must also carry our analysis one stage deeper, and see in the preceding centuries the incomplete dominance of Good Pagan culture over the partially civilized Barbarian.

We have thus three stages of progressive culture, and, inversely, three stages of corresponding reversion and regression.

In order to make our case comprehensible, we will first outline what, in our opinion, are the chief attributes of our Good Pagan and see to what extent these characteristics are, or are not, those of the civilization which, up till recent years, has been that of Western Europe, as opposed to what we may term Christian culture; we will then consider the Barbarian in his relation to our civilized Good Pagan, and see if this difference also corresponds, in any marked degree, to the changes which are generally acknowledged as typical of post-War society.

VI

In view of the different levels of paganism, it might seem more accurate to use "Humanist" as descriptive of our highly civilized Pagan, in opposition to Barbarian, but that word too has its own associations, it suggests a still more specialized form of the Good Pagan, the intellectual *par excellence*; our term must be of wider application, it must include the military virtues as well as those of intellectual value, the Latin super-imposed upon the Nordic.

Our Good Pagan is civilized, cultivated, reasonable, self-controlled. The qualities upon which he prides himself are essentially those that divide him from Barbarism. He is conscious of himself as representative of some kind of governing class, of an *élite*; he is an "Athenian," a "Roman," a "Gentleman," he may be a democratic Anglo-Saxon, he is still, as what he is, a superior being in opposition to something else unspecified. His representation is not automatic and determinate in the herd sense to which we have lately become accustomed, in the sense in which being Nordic or Proletarian is supposed to imply an automatic status. The Good Pagan's representative status is contingent on some quality in himself; it implies a point of honour, an obligation. "A So-and-So cannot lie," "a Spartan cannot retreat," may not be statements of fact, but they are statements of value.

The Greek word *Sophrosyne* is the essence of this Good Paganism. It is so Greek a word that it is hard to translate it; "moderation and wisdom," "kindness and good sense," is perhaps as near as we can get to it; if we put this beside the phrase *Mêden Agan*, "nothing too much," as the counsel of perfection, it is illuminating. With it goes always the sense of obligation, of duty towards oneself, one's neighbour, the community, of leading the "good life" as an end in itself, almost, one might say, for the sake of self-respect. The "good life" is envisaged as moderate, harmonious, balanced. The "polite" ideal of the eighteenth century is perhaps more superficial and external than the Athenian or even the Roman prototype, but it has much in common. *Surtout, pas trop de zèle*, is not far removed from *Mêden Agan*.

With this moderate ideal there goes a reasoned pride, not *Hubris* or "exaggerated pride"—that is eschewed at all costs, that is bad form, it is "not done" by the Good Pagan—but the "easy consciousness of effortless superiority," supposedly characteristic of the Balliol Man, is natural and suitable to all Good Pagans.

He has achieved and he knows it, why pretend? He is a

superior being compared with the outer world of Barbarians, and he knows it. He surpasses them in precisely those qualities which he most values and has been taught to value, in control and moderation and self-respect. He knows what is due to himself and to his neighbour and will, in so far as he lives up to his principles, take care to apportion their relative claims justly, but he will not be unfair to himself, or forgo his rights, why should he? Undue humility is as distasteful to him as *Hubris*. The attitude of the Publican in the Temple, would, if he heard of it, set his teeth on edge. Why call himself a sinner? Few are perfect. The Oriental exaggeration of such language is barbarous to him.

Now, does not all this apply, if we are honest, to the "English gentleman"? Are not his essential characteristics the same? I maintain that they are, that the parallel holds good in even secondary respects, and that the English gentleman is but one extreme example of the dominant governing class of Western Europe upon whose standards, and accepted values, we recognize our whole civilization to depend. The term "Christian gentleman" is still a term of respect, if partly amused and contemptuous respect, but I doubt if those who use it in this manner are aware of the deep paradox thus implied. The gentleman is guided by "good taste," a sense of what should be done, of what is fitting; in minor things, good form, in major, a sense of honour; this is surely mere transposition of what is *kalos*. He demands, and must demand, respect and deference as his due; he does not assert himself, is not aggressive, but he does take up the challenge that is offered. He is conscious of his own worth, and his duty to himself as representative of his own standard of behaviour. *Noblesse oblige* sums up this aspect of his code, his motive power, but the demands of *noblesse* are reasonable, his sense of honour is not exaggerated. He is "polite," *sophron*, and sensible. With him, as with the Christian, what he prizes is intangible, non-material; it is the idea of honour, of "the good," however flatly and uninspiringly he defines it; but, to him, the ideal is attainable, he has every expectation of reaching it, it is his fault and his disappointment if he fails to.

The Good Pagan and the Christian may often act in the same way, make the same moral judgments; they may both be virtuous, honourable and just, they may both be charitable and unselfish, they may be equally so, but the Pagan is satisfied, the Christian, not at all. The Pagan has attained his aim of the "good life," he is a man of honour, a good citizen, a good human being, he knows it and is content.

The Christian, on the other hand, measures himself by quite another standard, not in human excellence, but in relation to God. He is a citizen of another city. The idea of God becomes, to him, more real, more absorbing, in proportion as he himself draws nearer to Him. He is living his life as it were in a new dimension, in which the goodness he has attained seems negligible, non-existent, in comparison to the goodness he apprehends.

It is indeed notable that, the greater the Christian, the more nearly totalitarian in nature, the more does he suffer from a sense of sin, of imperfection, of inadequacy. It is easy to give examples of this truth:

> "As eyes weakened and clouded by humours suffer pain when the clear light beats upon them, so the soul by reason of its impurity suffers exceedingly when the Divine Light really shines upon it. And when the rays of this pure light strike upon the soul in order to expel its impurities, the soul perceives itself to be so unclean

and miserable that it seems as if God had set Himself against it, and it itself were set against God.

"The soul seeing distinctly in this bright and pure light, though dimly, its own impurity, acknowledges its own unworthiness before God and all creatures."[1]

"All the goodness of the whole world together, in comparison with the infinite goodness of God, is wickedness rather than goodness, for 'none is good but only God.' . . . .

"All the wisdom of the world, all human cunning, compared with the infinite wisdom of God, is simple and supreme ignorance, 'for the wisdom of this world is foolishness with God.' . . . .

"All the liberty and power of the world, compared with the power and liberty of the spirit of God, is but supreme slavery, wretchedness and captivity. . . ."[2]

"Miserable man that I am, what fellowship hath my perverseness with Thy uprightness? . . . . Thou art truly good, I wicked; Thou art full of compassion, I am hard of heart; Thou art holy, I am miserable; Thou art just, I am unjust; Thou art light, I am darkness; Thou art life, I am dead; Thou art medicine, I am sick; Thou art sovereign truth, I utter vanity."[3]

"It is the sight of God revealed to the eye of Faith that makes us hideous to ourselves from the contrast which we find ourselves to present to that great God at whom we look. It is the vision of Him in His infinite gloriousness, the All-Holy, the All-beautiful, the All-perfect, which makes us sink into the earth with self-contempt and self-abhorrence. We are contented with ourselves till we contemplate Him."[4]

These are not artificial sentiments nor pious efforts to edify. They are attempts on the part of these great Christians to

---

[1] St. John of the Cross, *Dark Night*, Bk. II, v. 6.
[2] *Ascent of Mount Carmel*, Bk. I, iv, 5, 6, 7.
[3] St. Augustine, *Soliloquy*, c. ii. Migne. P.L. XL, 866.
[4] Newman. *Sermons preached on Various Occasions*, 25. 9.

express in words what perhaps cannot be expressed, an apprehension of the fact of God.

If we compare these utterances of saints with equivalent statements from some representative Pagans, old and new, we shall see the extremity of their difference.

"The truth is, Athenians, that wherever a man's post may be, whether he has chosen it himself as the best place for him, or been set there by a superior, there it is his duty to remain at all risks, without thinking of death or of anything else except dishonour. When the officers whom you elected to be my superiors at Delium stationed me at my post, I stayed there, like anyone else, at the risk of death; and it would be strange if fear of death or anything whatever should make me a deserter now, when heaven, as I believe, has laid upon me the duty to spend my life in seeking wisdom and in examining myself and others. . . .

"To fear death is, in fact, to think you are wise when you are not; for it is to think you know what you do not know. No one knows whether death may not be the greatest good a man can have; yet men fear it as if they were certain it was the worst of evils. What is this but folly, that shameful folly of thinking we know what we do not know? Here again, I am perhaps superior to the ordinary man; if I were to make any claim to be wiser than others it would be because I do not think I have any sufficient knowledge of the other world, when in fact I have none. What I do know is that it is bad and dishonourable to do wrong and to disobey a superior, be he man or god. Accordingly, when I am confronted by evils which I know to be evils I will never take fright and run away from a thing which, for anything I know, may be a good."[1]

"At what employment then, would you have death find you? For my part, I would have it be some humane, beneficent public-spirited gallant action. But if I cannot

[1] Plato, *Apology*, 28ᴅ

be found doing any such great things, yet at least I would be doing what I am incapable of being restrained from, what is given to me to do, correcting myself, improving the faculty which makes use of the appearance of things, to procure tranquillity, and to render to the several relations of life their due; and, if I am so fortunate, advancing to the third topic, a security of judging right. If death overtakes me in such a situation, it is enough for me if I can stretch out my hands to God and say: 'The opportunities which Thou hast given me of comprehending and following the rules of Thy administration I have not neglected. As far as in me lay, I have not dishonoured Thee. See how I have used my perceptions, my preconceptions. Have I at any time found fault with Thee? Have I been discontented at Thy dispensations or wished them otherwise? Have I transgressed the relations of life? I thank Thee that Thou hast brought me into being. I am satisfied with the time that I have enjoyed, the things that Thou hast given me. Receive them back again and assign them to whatever place Thou wilt; for they were all Thine and Thou gavest them to me.' "[1]

"That Man is the product of causes which had no prevision of the end they were achieving; that his origin, his growth, his hopes and fears, his loves and his beliefs, are but the outcome of accidental collocations of atoms; that no fire, no heroism, no intensity of thought and feeling, can preserve an individual life beyond the grave; that all the labours of the ages, all the devotion, all the inspiration, all the noonday brightness of human genius, are destined to extinction in the vast death of the solar system, and that the whole temple of Man's achievement must inevitably be buried beneath the debris of a universe in ruins . . . all these things, if not quite beyond dispute, are yet so nearly certain, that no philosophy which rejects them can hope to stand. Only within the scaffold-

[1] Epictetus, *Discourses*. Bk. IV. Ch. x, cf. p. 76. St. Ignatius— same idea, but quite different emphasis.

ing of these truths, only on the firm foundation of un-yielding despair, can the soul's habitation henceforth be safely built.

" . . . The life of Man, viewed outwardly, is but a small thing in comparison with the forces of Nature. The slave is doomed to worship Time and Fate and Death, because they are greater than anything he finds in himself, and because all his thoughts are of things which they devour. But, great as they are, to think of them greatly, to feel their passionless splendour, is greater still. And such thought makes us free men; we no longer bow before the inevitable in Oriental subjection, but we absorb it and make it a part of ourselves. To abandon the struggle for private happiness, to expel all eagerness of temporary desire, to burn with passion for eternal things . . . this is emancipation, and this is the free man's worship. . . .

"Brief and powerless is Man's life; on him and all his race the slow sure doom falls pitiless and dark. Blind to good and evil, reckless of destruction, omnipotent matter rolls on its relentless way; for Man, condemned to-day to lose his dearest, to-morrow himself to pass through the gate of darkness, it remains only to cherish, ere yet the blow falls, the lofty thoughts that ennoble his little day; disdaining the coward terrors of the slave of Fate, to worship at the shrine that his own hands have built; undismayed by the empire of chance, to preserve a mind free from the wanton tyranny that rules his outward life; proudly defiant of the irresistible forces that tolerate, for a moment, his knowledge and his con-demnation, to sustain alone, a weary but unyielding Atlas, the world that his own ideals have fashioned despite the trampling march of unconscious power."[1]

[1] Bertrand Russell, *A Free Man's Worship.* Independent Review, Dec. 1938.

These extracts express the Good Pagan point of view in varying aspects of its higher forms; we may here compare with them an illustration of its later development.

Now are these two points of view compatible? Looked at objectively they are antagonistic, mutually exclusive, as world-outlooks, yet we all know rare and delightful individuals who do seem irrationally to combine them, who attain to the highest degree of *noblesse*, and pass on beyond; the Christian, as it were, transcends the gentleman. The whole medieval idea of chivalry is this. The knight of legend is in essence Christian, his knightly prowess is subservient to and contingent on his devotion; we need only consider the Grail Legend to realize it; yet we have condemned our civilization to failure because it attempted to combine the two; it is well to stop and consider for a moment the apparent contradiction in these views. It is our contention that our civilization was doomed to failure because what it attempted was wrongly balanced, the right

"Whether I have a conscience or not, I do not know, but certainly the traditional processes of moral conflict, the experiencing of temptation, the struggling against it, the succumbing to it and the subsequent remorse, or the overcoming it and the subsequent gain in moral 'kudos,' do not occur. Now I may be an unusual man; in some ways I dare say I am; but in this respect I cannot find that I am singular. For most of my generation seem to me to know no more of moral conflict than I do. They do not struggle against temptation ... most of them do not even know what it is ... their consciences do not fight for their souls against their passions, and they do not feel remorse. The whole apparatus of Victorian (sic.) moral machinery seems to be missing from their make-up; so much so that they are inclined to dismiss morality, as they are inclined to dismiss religion, as one of the many variants of nineteenth-century hypocrisy.... Our morality, in so far as we have one, is positive rather than negative. I consider it my duty to try to be a certain sort of person and to try to do certain things; but I cannot say that I think much about it one way or the other, and if on a given occasion I do not behave quite like the sort of person I would like to be, I do not think of myself as failing in my duty or betraying my ideal, and I certainly do not suffer remorse. For example, I recognize a certain obligation to keep my faculties tuned up to concert pitch. I wish to make the best use of such talents as I possess, ingredients were wrongly used. In the knight of the Grail we have an example of human prowess, strength, and *noblesse*, and physical courage, the impulse to right wrong, to reform the world, all in the service of God, dependent on it. There is no question at all of equal balance between a divine and human allegiance ultimately; he serves King Arthur as his earthly king, but neither he nor Arthur would suppose such earthly kingship should compete with God.

In the enlightened Pagan of liberalism, the position is reversed. Earthly allegiance to the Human Race, to Man as ultimate, has supplanted Divine allegiance. The Christian ethic is in part preserved because it is found to be of use to Man. What of the Christian values are retained, are retained in exact proportion to this test. It is Man that arbitrates,

---

to develop my powers to the full and to keep myself generally at the highest pitch of efficiency of which I am capable. I want, in a word, to realize all that I have it in me to be. Accordingly, I regard it as my business to achieve and maintain as high a standard of mental and bodily health as I can compass without serious discomfort. . . . In spite of what I have said to the contrary, I find, on reflection, that there is, after all, one set of circumstances in which I do experience moral conflict. I experience temptation, fight against it, suffer remorse if I succumb to it, and give way to complacency if I overcome it. But the circumstances are not those traditionally associated with moral endeavour. I have a horror of cruelty to animals. The feeling, no doubt, is virtuous and does me credit, but it is violent and irrational in its expression, and, on the whole, I am ashamed of it, or at least of my inability to control it. . . . I cannot bear to go to the Zoo and I cannot endure the spectacle of performing animals. The existence of the Zoo seems to me an outrage in a civilized society. An eagle in a cage is a terrible sight, and the lifelong imprisonment of lions and tigers equally degrading to prisoners and jailers. The Roman lions did at least have a Christian breakfast; the prisoners of the Zoo have only the myriad, merciless eyes of their secure captors, gazing, gazing, gazing until the flesh rots and the heart breaks in the respectable prison."—*The Book of Joad*, by C. E. M. Joad, Ch. xi.

Man that chooses what of God's things may be of use to him. This is surely "to change the truth of God into a lie, and worship and serve the creature more than the Creator."

It is our contention that there is no true value which cannot be included in the Christian value, nothing of ultimate use to human beings which has no part in the Divine Order, but it must take its place in its right order; the lower cannot function for the higher, Man cannot govern God for his own purpose.

To class Christianity, as is sometimes done, as a Proletarian Religion, suited for and formed by the needs of the oppressed, is a grossly one-sided and misleading judgment, it is to distort and impoverish the whole, yet it is clearly true that its first appeal is to the down-trodden and the helpless, and the history of the early Church demonstrates it. It is easier for a poor man to accept its implications; in it, he has all to gain, nothing to lose. This is no new reflection; we need only remember the young ruler with great possessions, or the camel and the needle's eye, to know that this has been explicit from the beginning.

It is harder for members of a governing class to be Christian, for they are, *qua* governing class, in a privileged position which they must, as it were, discount and offer up as their entrance fee. Their position of privilege in a Pagan world is a Pagan one, and depends in the last resort on values they must relinquish or supersede. They may, and probably must, continue in these positions, exerting the same authority, exacting in some sense the same respect, but without the satisfaction and sense of merit which has been a material part of their position.

It is often lamented that in our present Barbarian proletarian society the sense of personal pride in achievement has been lost, that the element of merit and prowess has been eliminated from work by the machine; that this is true and deplorable, we admit; according to the measure of Good Paganism, on which we maintain our society to be based, such pride is right and wholesome, and essential; to lose it, in any case, as we are now losing it, simply from indifference and negligence, is clearly an evolutionary regression, yet the Christian standpoint does demand a giving up, in a totally different way, of this same good, whose loss we are now deploring, but a giving it up from the opposing pole, not by slackening of tension, but by intensification, not by undervaluing this, but by a greater value of something else. Again a question of relativity.

I must at the same time value my achievement, make efforts to achieve it, and be worthy of my status when achieved, and yet know it of no value, as conferring no merit at all upon me, in another dimension, in which, it may be, I am less worthy than the subject over whom, I am, rightly, in authority. This is not merely difficult, it is in a sense against nature; the Pagan upper-class revolt is not surprising; the Christian gentleman is a *tour de force*, but the difficulty of an achievement is very often a measure of its value.

We must, I think, conclude that these two points of view, in themselves it is true contradictory, can be inexplicably combined, can ultimately be brought into harmony, fused, or perhaps transfused is a better word; that it has been done, and can be done, and is done, but that to do so successfully is hard, that it makes demands on the individual and on his society from which both society and individual often shrink; yet they do not readily admit that they do so; the use of "Christian" as a synonym for "civilized" is proof of this, yet it is precisely those people and classes of people to whom to be civilized comes most easily and naturally, that find to be Christian the most difficult and unnatural. The problem that confronts us is no new one; St. Augustine has described our "Christian gentleman."

> "We see now a citizen of Jerusalem, a citizen of the Kingdom of Heaven, holding some office upon earth; as, for example, wearing the purple, serving as a magistrate, as aedile, as proconsul, as Emperor directing the earthly republic, but he has his heart above, if he is a Christian; if he is of the faithful, he despiseth these things wherein he is, and trusteth in that wherein he is not yet."[1]

Now, accepting the fact that it is not the same thing to be civilized as to be Christian, that the two points of view we have been trying to define are, although they can be fused, in themselves opposed, can we doubt which, in fact, has been active as the motive force in our own modern pre-War society? Which standard prevailed, or at any rate was encouraged, in our great public schools, in our universities, in our Government? How many times would the thought: "it is un-Christian," have restrained the average man from a course of action, when "a gentleman couldn't do it," would have restrained him? I put my question purposely in the past tense, for we start from the assumption that the pre-War order, whatever its true nature, is past, or in process of passing, that the standards and sanctions on which it was built are no longer counting in the world to-day.

VII

We have shown, or tried to show, in the preceding pages, how largely the Good Pagan characteristics are those of our own modern pre-War world, how largely they have formed the mental outlook of the active governing class of Western Europe, of the class which governed until recently. The ideas

[1] St. Augustine. *Enarrationes in Psalmos*, li, 6.

which characterize a governing class do in fact affect the entire population; adapted perhaps, and modified and diluted, they operate through the whole society. If we are satisfied that, at least in a large measure, the culture which formed us has been a Pagan culture, we are still left with the unanswered question as to how far, in fact, it has ever been non-Pagan?

We have already cited, as an example of Christian dominance, the reception accorded throughout Europe to St. Bernard, and compared it to its present-day substitute, the world-recognition accorded to a film star. Let us try to pursue this line of inquiry further, to define more exactly what we mean by Christian, what quality it was in St. Bernard's populace which is lacking in the public opinion of to-day.

In this connection, we are speaking of Europe and, in especial, Western Europe, which is the essential home of the civilization we know. It is quite beyond the scope of this inquiry to consider equivalent problems in other parts of the world. For our purpose, and in regard to Europe, Christianity can be taken as synonymous with religion; I use it in that sense, with no disrespect to other religious systems which may share to a greater or less degree in some of the characteristics that we shall define as Christian. We are justified therefore in using the term Christian as though there were no other real religion; for us in Western Europe, at any rate, there is not.

We have already considered the Good Pagan; we have seen that he is moderate, rational, self-controlled, that he values justice and a sense of duty, that he has a moral code which he, on the whole, obeys. Are we then to deduce that, in contrast to him, the Christian is lacking in those qualities? That he is immoderate, uncontrolled, does not care about justice or duty, that he has no moral code, or that, if he has, he does not live up to it?

This, as it stands, would be an absurd deduction, and yet I think it is not altogether absurd; I think that that is in fact how the Christian does appear to the Good Pagan; he often shocks him, and outrages his moral sense, in addition to his sense of "what is fitting"; and this is interesting, for to know how others see us, often tells us a great deal about ourselves.

Let us then consider the accusations, one by one:

Immoderate, exaggerated, what do we mean by that?

It all depends on our standard of moderation. Nobody, not even the most philosophic Pagan, can really demand moderation in everything, not in virtue, for instance, nor in integrity, nor in wisdom; no Christian, on the other hand, would wish to be immoderate or exaggerated if he thought about it, but the standards of what was, or was not, exaggerated would seem to each different, and their degree of importance would be different.

When St. Francis and Brother Ruffino walked through the streets, half naked, with their habits rolled up in bundles on their heads, they did not do so from love of "immoderation," they did so because they were thinking in other terms altogether; their value was not a moderation-value, and the question of "sweet reasonableness" did not enter into their calculations at all.

To claim, as is sometimes done, that all the exaggerated elements in Christianity are extraneous, that they are, in fact, a pity, and non-essential, is merely an attempt to combine two incompatibles, to get the best of both worlds by losing both.

That the "element of exaggeration" is intrinsic to Christianity, we have only to read St. Paul's Epistles to see, and the effect his great speech made on the Athenians shows how it struck a real Pagan audience.

Lack of moderation is a negative expression, and inadequate;

it is rather some very positive term we need; limitless, bound-less, infinite, extreme, intense—none of these words contains the entirety—even our words are framed in the Pagan mould. Moderate has become itself the positive word; immoderate is only what is not moderate, and this is misleading if we consider their real meaning. The nearest we can get as a defini-tion is probably to say it in terms of some definite quality; if we take "moderation in heat" as our example, we may say that the Pagan aim is tepidity, the Christian aim is always hot or cold. The Pagan who blames St. Simeon for being im-moderate is like someone blaming the cook for boiling the kettle, on the ground that the water will lose its tepidity.

Self-control is in some respects in a different category; both Pagan and Christian would approve it, but they would, I think, mean rather different things. The Stoic self-control is negative, it is an end in itself, and leads us nowhere, the Christian asceticism is again more active, it is a means to an end, it is sharing in the suffering of Christ, it is taking the offensive against the Devil; again, it is heat or cold as against tepidity. To the Pagan, the Christian ascetic seems uncon-trolled, he seems "giving way" to remorse, to hysteria, because the end in view is unperceived. The difference is real, and they misjudge each other.

Love of justice: here again, the misunderstanding is deep. The Christian strikes the Pagan as indifferent to justice; he often takes less trouble to right abuses, he is apt to show less indignation at oppression or cruelty, he does not bother enough about putting the world to rights, and this is deeply shocking to the Pagan, to whom all these things stand for love of justice.

Yet the Christian, too, would claim that he loved justice, he would perhaps claim that he loved it more, but justice for him would consist in different things. He would not say that cruelty and oppression did not matter, but he would say that they were not ultimate; he would say that how you endured or faced an evil was more important than the evil itself, that the sum of all material evil was of less matter than one venial sin, that the final value was not here or now.

The life of St. Peter Claver gives a good example of this attitude. He worked for thirty years among the slaves in Cartagena, through the cruellest and most heart-rending phase of the slave trade; he gave himself utterly to the service of slaves, living and working among them, sharing their intolerable conditions, to save their souls, but, so far as one can learn, he made no attempt to stop the trade. There are many cases like his that one could quote, and they are "to the Jews a stumbling block, and to the Greeks folly."

We see from this analysis that the Pagan is to some extent justified in his accusation that the Christian is not concerned with moderation; it is not enough, he is after something more; that he is not concerned with the negative self-control the Pagan values; it is not enough, he is after something more; that he is not concerned very much with concrete justice; he wants it, it is true, and often, far oftener than the Pagan realizes, it is he who has brought it about in the actual world, but it is not enough for him, he is after something more.

In each case we see, if we look at it in this way, not a difference of opinion so much as of degree, of intensity; what satisfies the Pagan leaves the Christian unsatisfied, his value is not bounded by these things; here we have found the intrinsic difference; where the treasure is, there will the heart be also, and the Christian, as such, has an "other-worldly" treasure.

This world and its doings, its justice or injustice, its moderation and common sense, its wisdom or folly, is not to him, *qua* Christian, of first importance, it is relative to, contingent on, something else, on a greater, more real world of other values, with which he believes himself to be in contact, which he apprehends, fleetingly, intermittently, it may be, but on whose existence, through and behind this world of sense, his own existence, as Christian, must depend. He is living always in a fifth-dimensional world, and the existence of this fifth dimension changes and transmutes the other four.

He is like someone listening; he shuts his eyes at times to catch the faint sounds from a distance; having heard them once or twice, or even oftener, he knows that they are there, if he cannot always hear them, and this makes him tiresome and exasperating to the Good Pagan, to whom such sounds are delusion, auto-suggestions, or faery music, according to the age in which he lives.

Why waste one's time on perhaps harmful nonsense, when there are slums to clear and drains to lay?

The advantages of the Pagan attitude are obvious; the slums are there to be cleared, we can all see them, the drains are there to be laid, we cannot deny them; it is good, quite clearly and demonstrably, that they should be laid and cleared, and the other world of the Christian is non-apparent; how can we know that he is not mistaken, that he is not in fact exchanging substance for shadow, like the dog with a bone in Aesop's fable, dropping the actual bone for a reflection?

It is an accusation against religion that it tends to flourish under bad conditions, but this fact need not surprise us nor confuse us. It is always easier for other-worldly values to gain recognition when times are bad and this world's prospects are doubtful. When our own city is falling, we are more ready to place our treasure in the City of the Sun. We find, as we should expect, that the Christian attitude has been strongest in the times when material life was hardest, and security in this world least assured.. That fact tells us nothing new about either Christianity or Paganism, it only re-affirms our knowledge of human nature, the characteristic weakness of the natural man.

It is clearly more difficult to take long views than short ones, to accept intangible values rather than tangible; if a quick reward is offered on easy terms, most of us are tempted to take it. It needs less will power, less tenacity of purpose, to push on through the Sahara to our objective, than to push on as unhaltingly through a fertile valley. Where no sirens tempt us, why should we approach the rocks? It is therefore with no surprise that we find the Pagan values re-asserting themselves in prosperity.

The fifteenth and sixteenth centuries, with the discovery of the new world, the expansion of the material boundaries of Europe, new learning, new commerce, new inventions, the printing press, bigger ships, greater ease of travel, were conspicuously such a time. The prizes that this world offered were overwhelming; the sense of power and mastery, man's conquest of his environment—this has always been one of the strongest forces in Paganism—the exultant triumph of the natural man. And again, we must be honest, which of us does not respond to such achievement? Which of us, if we give rein to our natural impulse, does not thrill to the great chorus of Sophocles:

"Wonders are many, but none there be,
So strange, so fell, as the Child of Man.
He rangeth over the whitening sea,
Of the winds of Winter he makes his plan.
About his going, the deeps unfold,
The crests o'erhang, but he passeth clear;

Oh Earth is patient, Earth is old,
And a mother of Gods, but he breaketh her.
To-ing and fro-ing, with the plough teams going,
Tearing the soil of her year by year.

Speech he hath taught him, and wind-swift thought,
And the temper that buildeth a City's wall
Till the arrows of Winter he sets at naught,
The sleepless cold and the long rainfall.
All-armèd he; unarmèd never,
To meet new peril he journeyeth;
Yea, his craft assuageth each pest that rageth,
And help he hath gotten against all save death."[1]

And in this mood, when we are still tired with successful effort, when we stand back and "see that it is good," how repellent seems the folly of the Cross! We are fine fellows, and we know we are!

This period of expansion and achievement has in fact lasted for four hundred years. The spirit of Paganism, the triumphant natural man, has asserted itself through the whole life of Europe with varying degrees of articulate self-expression.

The Renaissance, the Reformation, the French Revolution, the Encyclopædists, which were but a precursor of it, the Industrial Revolution, the Nationalist upheavals of the nineteenth century, are all merely varying expressions of one spirit, all self-assertion of the natural man: "This is human, this is natural, this is ME!" they are all shouting, and, up to a point, they do achieve their object, they do impress their power upon their environment.

During these four hundred years of Pagan dominance, the material conditions of life have improved immeasurably. We hear so much talk of mechanical progress that our ears are

[1] *Antigone* 332-375—translated by Gilbert Murray.

blunted and we almost forget about it, but it is real, and, in itself, astounding.

The conditions of housing, yes, even with slum conditions, of health, of communications, of pleasure and entertainment, the degree to which these advantages are available to the poor, the change in prison conditions, in the treatment of the insane, the abolition of torture and barbarous punishments, all these are real, and most of the credit must go to the Good Pagan. He has concentrated, as was to be expected, entirely on his own world of immediate values, the whole energy of twelve generations has gone to the improvement of this world, and it has improved out of all recognition, in those things, in those ways, on which he has concentrated.

But the Christian still exists. He has existed through all these four hundred years, and he has not ceased his disconcerting query:

"Is it worth while, all this that you are doing? Moth and rust will still corrupt, thieves will still break through and steal; you are getting nowhere, you are achieving nothing; four hundred miles an hour will not get you to Heaven quicker; you cannot tune in to Eternity by radio."

And because, as we said, there is, in everybody, something of both kinds of mind, the Christian in every Pagan responds uneasily:

"Yes, what about it?" he urges. "Do you hear what he is saying?"

And the Pagan in himself will answer firmly:

"It is nonsense; there is nowhere that we cannot reach in time. If Heaven is anywhere, we are bound to get there."

The Christian and the Pagan are at cross purposes. They live in the same world—very often, as we have seen, in the same person—yet one is always hostile to the other. At one time, one predominates, at another, the other, but so long as both exist each must be threatened; in the long run there can be no room for both.

Each belittles and denies the other's value, each counts the other's labour waste of time.

In warfare or conflict of any kind it is natural to misjudge one's adversary, the Christian ought to love his enemy. The Pagan demands less of himself, we know, but he would claim to judge his enemy justly. In practice, both fall short of their ideal; both are unfair and deny the other's worth. Each one sees the other as enemy not of himself alone, but of the "good."

Can we detach ourselves sufficiently, for the moment, to see these opposing forces in perspective, to assess at all their relative strength and weakness, giving attention to the claims of both? It is this that we will attempt in the following pages.

VIII

The danger of the Christian point of view is withdrawal, a turning of the mind from active life, an abandonment of the world to its destruction, which can show itself in many different ways. This tendency is reinforced in the world to-day by the minority sense which all Christians have, at least in sophisticated Western Europe. The predominant atmosphere is so acutely hostile to any other-worldly valuation that the individual, or even the group, that defends the other-worldly point of view, is pressed very easily into exaggeration.

The sense of the Pagan world's overpowering force, of the hopelessness of making headway against it, turns him in on himself perhaps too much, or at least on his own exclusive circle of the elect.

There comes a point in world affairs where such a defensive

attitude is essential, where to keep a small undamaged light still burning is all that can be demanded of the Faithful. Such an attitude is not in the least self-centred, as it is judged by prevalent world opinion, but it does in effect admit a losing battle in terms of here and now; it is dependent on much longer views, and the modern world insists on quick returns. Our forefathers planted oak-trees, knowing well that neither they nor their sons nor their grandsons would reap the benefit of mature timber; now it is thought absurd to look so to the future. We cut down the oaks that our forbears planted, and we plant instead only firs that should be ripe for felling in our own life time; this is surely typical of much besides.

This withdrawal was necessary in the Dark Ages; it became impossible for the Christian to live his life in the world as it had become. The obstacles to the "good life" were too over-whelming; only in the monasteries was such life practicable, only there was culture of any sort safeguarded and passed on to the world in better times. Such conditions may prevail again in Europe; it is possible that another Dark Age is in sight when all immaterial values will be denied, all participation in the active life of nations become impossible for Christian people.

The exact moment at which such a situation does arise is difficult to define. For a Christian living in Russia, it has arisen; in Germany, very nearly, if not quite; in Spain it has been in sight, and we do not know the future; but there is clearly a danger of defeatism, a danger of mistaking inaction for patience, and sloth for wisdom. If the believing Christians in the world to-day had the courage and activity that their Faith demands, small as their numbers are, they would prevail, or, at least, in far greater measure than they are, they would be a force in the counsels of the world. There is a danger, always, of "quietism," and passivity is not faith. The inaction and ineffectiveness of Christians is the gravest accusation of the Good Pagan and the hardest to meet.

"If what you believe is true," he says, "or even if it is only really true to you, you ought to be so much better than I am, so much stronger and more effective than I can ever be, and in practice it is seldom that you are."

The only answer to this accusation is that the real Christian, when we find him, is both better and far stronger than the Pagan, but he is rare. The great mass of so-called Christians are half-hearted, half at least of their true allegiance is Pagan, and the house divided against itself must fall.

Most people, as we have seen already, have both in them. We recognize both elements in ourselves, and this makes it much harder to separate the warring and incompatible elements.

The Christian is far more Pagan than he knows; the Pagan is more Christian than he admits.

IX

The principal weakness of the Good Pagan lies in the unreality of his *Weltanschauung*, the illusion on which he rests his whole position, but if we have to pick out a chief example of how this unreality is manifested, we should say that it was in his response to evil, to pain and failure and sin. We should say that he has the narrowness of outlook which is characteristic of the aristocrat; the only world he knows, is his own world.

He is at home in a picked society, in an oligarchic and exclusive circle where he moves among his peers and rules the mob. His virtues are the virtues of the few, of the governing class. He can live with gentlemen like himself and understand them; in a civilized world he can be supreme; the degree of his supremacy is, perhaps, a test of civilization—but at no time has the world been all civilized. In society and in individual alike, there are, and always have been, barbaric forces, violent, elemental, and untamed; there are, and always have been, conflicts and agonies, fears and despairs, inabilities to face death, or cope with life; and against these forces the Good Pagan, as such, is helpless.

His helplessness in this respect is twofold; in his life as a social being, in relation to unredeemed suffering humanity in the world, and a counterpart of this, when things go wrong with him, in relation to the unredeemed suffering human in himself.

He can counsel wisdom, he can exhort to courage, he can, in his own case, endure heroically, but he cannot save, and so, in the last resort, to a world needing salvation, he is useless, and he is repudiated, with all that he stands for, the good that he did along with his shortcomings; his morality, his magnanimity, his moderation, all are now swept away.

They asked him for bread and he has given them stones; they have no patience, no time for his defence.

This is, we submit, the present situation; this is the explanation of what has happened, the revolt of the Barbarian, with all its consequences.

The greatest challenge with which we are all faced, in some form or other, at some time or other, in our lives as individuals, and in our social lives, is this challenge of evil and failure, of the sinner, the barbarian, the outcast. A system of life into which he cannot fit, which ignores him and the element in us all that he represents, cannot endure.

Paganism has failed in relation to the outcast, and, by its failure here, it stands condemned.

X.

We have suggested in the foregoing pages that the present world crisis, the downfall of civilization, is due to the failure of the Good Pagan culture which has been the culture of civilized Western Europe for the last four hundred years. In our definition of Pagan culture we have tried to emphasize its positive moral basis, the large measure of ethical value which it shares with Christianity, the reason we have for feeling, and feeling rightly, that the present revolt against it is deplorable and dangerous, and to be resisted. We have finally indicated what, in our opinion, is the key to so catastrophic a collapse; the failure of the Good Pagan's response to evil.

The Good Pagan we have depicted so far, the philosopher, the stoic, the aristocrat, is an ideal, he is almost, in fact, as rare as the good Christian. It is arguable that in his pure form he could have steered humanity to some reasonable degree of good existence, in spite of the weakness that we find in him, but that line of argument we need not follow. If there were enough people who were good enough, our problems would solve themselves; what we must try to find in this connection is rather what elements in this Pagan goodness have in fact led to its failure. Is the failure fortuitous, a bit of bad luck that might have been averted? Or is it rather an inherent weakness, an error, a false assumption on which it rests? If this last is true, as we believe it to be, can we trace out the error in its working, and link up the fundamental kink convincingly with its manifestation? Does the way things have worked out really correspond with the way they would work out on our supposition? We hold that it does.

In approaching this question of the failure of the Good Pagan, we shall pick out different elements of failure according

to our personal *Weltanschauung*. The Good Pagan civilization, as we have known it, is roughly the liberal, rationalist
"enlightenment." Everybody is agreed upon its failure, even its
adherents are in agreement there, but we shall all offer different
explanations.

The Communist sees the failure of capitalism, of *laissez
faire* in economic life, and the individualistic basis of society;
all these were there, it is true and it has failed.

The Fascist sees the failure of liberalism, of humanitarian
sentiment, and lack of discipline; all these were there, it is true,
and it has failed.

The Christian sees the materialistic basis, a denial of supernatural value, the "anthropocentric" focussing of life; all
these were there as well, and it has failed.

There may be truth in all these criticisms, they are not
necessarily contradictory, but even if we are able to agree so
far, we shall attach such different emphasis to the different
accusations that our agreement becomes insignificant.

The Good Pagan has failed; his regime is over; and with him
goes, for most of the intellectual governing class in Europe, the
value and the amenities of life. The world is relapsing into
barbarism; the Good Pagan, the Gentleman cannot survive.

In considering the defeat of the Good Pagan there are two
distinct aspects we should consider:

(1) The weakness of the Good Pagan in his highest
examples.

(2) The demoralization and degradation of the Good Pagan.

The first we have already considered; we have noted that
in his best examples the Good Pagan stands for idealism of a
high degree, for an ultimate, intangible goodness value, which
is far removed from the mass-production standard of to-day;
is it therefore fair to lay the blame on him for the barbarization

that we now complain of? I think that, in spite of apparent contradiction, it is.

The barbarization of life, as we now see it, is essentially the supplanting of higher, less tangible values, by solider, more immediate returns. This process has been intensified recently by the increased mechanization of life, the supplanting of human skill by the machine, but it is in its essence only the same process as the transference of value from God to Man, which is the essential basis of the Pagan. The philosophic Pagan has taken the first step when he removes his treasure from Heaven to this world, when he substitutes the service of Man, *qua* Man, for the service of God through service of our neighbour. The first step does not seem, perhaps, important, he is still serving some one not himself, preferring a distant good to immediate self-satisfaction, but the movement has begun, without his realization of what is happening; the cart has begun to run away down the hill.

It is true that in the first instance the emphasis does not seem to be ego-centric; he may indeed spend himself in philan-thropies; but he has, for better or worse, removed his treasure from what is above and other than himself, to what is, essentially, himself projected.

The relation of Man to God is one of humility, of inequality, a consciousness of man's dependence on something else, the contingent nature of human power, a kind of spiritual relativity. The repudiation of God is the reversal of this emphasis; it is, in essence, aggressive, it is the self-assertion of mankind, the claim to equalitarian independence, and you cannot in practice check the aggressive movement; it appeals to too fundamental a rebellion.

If I claim for myself and my kind the supremacy that once belonged to God, I am started on the road of self-assertion; if

I am "instead of" God, "as good as" God, I am most certainly, "as good as" you. The whole emphasis of development becomes aggressive. The religious conception of life is hierarchic, a service of higher by lower, all playing their parts, all having their different parts to play. The emphasis is essentially on serving, on obedience, on doing what you suppose the will of God for you, rather than assertion of your own will, and increasingly, in proportion to the religious motive, is the emphasis on God's will as opposed to mine. It is life as a pattern, a harmony, a design, in which each line, each curve, each note is needed, but it demands acceptance of unequal functions, an acquiescence in inequality.[1]

The Good Pagan demanded the impossible when he pushed the cart over the hill, and over the brow, and told it to stop half-way down. He dethroned God and put Man in His place, and then demanded the hierarchic pattern: "You shall all play equal parts, you shall all co-operate." But it did not work, because it could not work; the orchestra could not play with no conductor; who should play what? At what pace should they play? So it began and so it has continued, the equalitarian disintegration.

Everyone wishes to be the right-hand angle, everyone wishes to play first violin, but with only right-hand angles there is no pattern, with only first violins, no symphony.

The resultant chaos could not be avoided if once the Pagan's view of life prevailed; such development was intrinsic in his outlook, though he himself did not envisage it.

[1] In the later ancient Pagan philosophy, the idea of life as design or harmony prevailed. The Stoic's insistence on submission of the individual will to the Divine Harmony is almost Christian, and Plato asserts as vital the relation of parts to whole—but in these we see approach and not rejection; they were moving nearer to the Christian outlook, through experience of catastrophe in this world. The triumphant spirit of fifth-century Athens is the parallel to our post-Christian Paganism.

In every revolution we have known there is an attempt by some moderate party to hold in check the forces they have released, and always the moderates are swept aside by more violent and more extreme examples of the movement they themselves have started. This is what has happened now to the Good Pagan, being swamped and overwhelmed by barbarism. It is not only in the social sense that this movement has prevailed, but the mechanization of mind, which we have seen to be characteristic of it, has permeated all the social fabric; the Good Pagan himself has been infected by it; he had and has no resistance to offer; he has himself become materialized.

We must here distinguish between two different aspects of Pagan culture, two stages rather in that view of life, the philosophic or moral attitude and the scientific or mechanistic. We have so far considered chiefly the former, and it is, I believe, at bottom the more important because it is closer to the religious view; it is, as it were, the departure point, the dividing of the ways, where, as it now seems, we have chosen wrongly. The various later developments from this are all dependent, ultimately, upon it, but the scientific mechanistic view has loomed so large, especially in our day, that it has claimed almost a separate place. It is this form, this degeneration, of Pagan idealism that has largely superseded the philosophic in the mind of the average educated man, and it is undoubtedly a debased form of this that has caught alight in the barbarian mind.

We should consider, in this context, the effect of the machine upon its maker; the machine is a product of the scientific mind, the greater the individual scientist, the less is he bound by his own mechanism, but the laws which, to him, are tools to work with, become, to his weaker brethren, cramping chains. He has, when we look at him objectively, merely narrowed the spiritual horizon one stage further, he has shut us in more closely on ourselves, in the present world.

Looking at it from this angle, we can see the development of our Good Pagan civilization as one long progress of diminishing horizons.

We hear to-day of the expanding universe; is this perhaps the necessary reaction from generations progressively limited in outlook and potentiality? The material universe may be expanding; the spiritual universe has been contracting; the scientist is natural heir to the philosopher.

The philosopher dethroned God, in favour of Sovereign Man, the scientist dethroned Man in favour of Animal Nature, and finally even the animal is now yielding to the Machine.

At each stage, the field of our existence contracts yet further, from man to beast, from live beast to dead machine, and when once we realize what has been happening, we see that this development is natural, it accords with the natural weakness of our nature. If it is, as it is, a natural characteristic to choose the easier way when it is offered, to avoid effort and difficulty unless the inducement to face them is overwhelming, we can see that this contracting universe offers the line of least resistance to us. The less scope for action we have, the smaller will be the demands that are made upon us. More is expected of the supernatural man than of the natural man, more of the natural man than of the animal, more of the animal than of the machine. Viewing it in this light, we see it as regression, the relapse from a higher form of life to a lower form. It stands to reason then that indolence, the natural tendency to take it easy, will operate against the supernatural.

It is commonly said that religion, like magic, is a short-cut means for avoiding healthy effort; it depends, of course, on

what is meant by religion; it is possible for the religious sense
to degenerate into a form of magic in which all values and
faculties succumb, but it is clear that a real apprehension of
long-distance values against immediate gains is symptomatic
of a higher culture, as with the growing child it is a sign of
progress when the immediate object of desire gives way to
future and distant wishes. The stage in which we seize and
eat what pleases us is less developed than the abstinence of
the young athlete in training. The fact that his desire is long-
distance, to excel in the race some weeks or months ahead, is
acknowledged to be a higher state demanding from him
powers that we admire. The parallel holds good in many
ways, for if every one tells the boy that he is silly, that the
race, when it comes off, is of no importance, and that perhaps
there will never be any race at all, can we expect him to go
on just the same, giving up his immediate pleasures, his sweets
and his cigarettes, for the sake of a test that is so depreciated?
He certainly will not, and the result is to drive him back into the
childish stage, from which with an effort he was just emerging.

This surely is the psychologist's "regression," which we
are assured brings all our ills.[1]

XI

We can see this same progressive deterioration in the attempt
of our Pagan civilization to deal with sin, or what in another
age would be termed sin.

[1] Cf., C. E. M. Joad, *Book of Joad*, p. 271.
  "Why keep myself fit if I do not know for what my fitness is
required? Why tune up my faculties if I do not play upon them?
Only a Puritan embitters his life with preparations for a race that
is never run."
Mr. Joad's conclusion from these statements is not ours, but his
reasoning so far is in agreement.

We have said that the weakness of the Pagan outlook is shown most clearly in its failure to deal with suffering unredeemed humanity; this is, we admit, the hardest test to all systems of thought, all views of the universe.

The Christian approaches the subject unembarrassed, for the Fall of Man is assumed in his position. The perverseness, the blindness of fallen human nature is the basis on which his *Weltanschauung* rests. In so far as he is a wholehearted Christian, he has a message directly for the fallen; the fact that the sinner is bad or stupid, or both, does not upset his case, it strengthens it. In the great pattern of life, as he sees it, even the sinner, as such, has his place:

"*O certe necessarium Adae peccatum quod Christi morte deletum est;*
O felix culpa, quae talem ac tantum meruit habere redemptorem!"

The salvation which he preaches, assumes sin; to him, God Himself is incarnate in the outcast.

But the whole idea of redemption is in the Xth dimension, as we might call the supernatural order. When you abolish God and eternity you abolish redemption, but you do not thereby abolish the need for it. The Good Pagan is left with his unredeemed humanity, and it does not and will not fit into his pattern of life.

When the philosopher admits himself defeated, he invites the man of science to try his hand.

Man is an animal, a physical being, and must be treated as such; the philosopher's failure is to him a foregone conclusion; all mental states have physical origins, we must attack the source of the disease. He founds health services, and clinics and remedial centres, he takes out their teeth and their appendices, he feeds them with vitamins and treats them with rays; he is sure that if their bodies function rightly, all will be right, he will not say "good," for that word has associations that he rejects, but they will get rid of their anti-social tendencies— but somehow it does not work. The sinner is still there, though now he is called a social misfit, or a patient. He is ungrateful and obstinate when you offer to try yet another cure upon him.

He will not fit into the scientist's life pattern any more than he fitted into the philosopher's, and the scientist loses patience too, and averts his mind.

We see the logical outcome of these failures in the movements for sterilization and euthanasia. Failures do not fit in, they must be liquidated; we must get rid of them and forget about them. As animals, that is true of the unfit, but where should such measures stop? How many of us then should be kept alive? How many of us doubters do not fit in? Shall we not soon come to the logical abolition of all heretics?

The wonders of science, applied and unapplied, continue to stagger our imaginations, the cures of diseases supposedly incurable, are there, and we should be foolish and ungrateful to minimize them, but it does not seem that people are growing better from the old-fashioned moral point of view. We have only to read any modern novel to see that the old bad human nature motives are assumed as much as, or perhaps more than, they ever were. It is only that they are no longer condemned as bad.

We used to be told that people would be happy so soon as they could get free from inhibitions, from the artificial moral repressions which the old moral laws imposed upon them; now they have freed themselves amazingly, and with increasing speed, but are they happy?

The director of a psychological institute has lately drawn our attention to the fact that the rate of successful suicide in England and Wales to-day, is about one every hour and a half. That does not suggest a happy population.

It will not work, the Good Pagan *Weltanschauung*.

II

THE UNITED FRONT

"The Lord thy God shalt thou adore, and Him only shalt thou serve."

—MATT. iv.

I

We have been considering in our earlier pages some aspects
of the two rival attitudes to life, what we have called the "Good
Pagan" and the "Christian." We have shown that our own
civilization consists in a fusion, or confusion, of the two; in
name it is largely Christian, at heart, Pagan. We have shown
that, even in the individual, the pure type of either is extremely
rare; the Pagan is more Christian than he knows, the Christian
far more Pagan than he suspects. We have seen how the
Christian idea of life conquered Europe without penetrating
to its inner depth; how the older forms of Pagan *Weltanschauung*
persisted underneath the Christian surface and how, in the
centuries of our modern era, they have been increasingly
penetrating upward, transforming what we still call our
Christian civilization into an almost entirely Pagan culture.

We are all familiar with this process in conquests of one
race by another; in India, in Ancient Greece we have seen it
happen, the incoming dominant race, the conqueror keeps in
name his position and his dominance, but in practice his type
is soon obliterated, the indigenous racial type dilutes and
swamps him while taking on his name and his prestige.

This process has gone so far in our day in the mental or
moral or spiritual field that we are in serious danger of forgetting the very nature of our two ideas.

There have been in the past very great disasters, through
too sharp a realization of the difference; this conflict of ideas
has been too acute and has torn civilization apart and wounded

it, almost, at times it has seemed, mortally. There are signs of a return to such violence to-day, but in the meantime, and still principally, in the most civilized democratic countries, in the parts of our world which still retain to any appreciable degree the character of the enlightened liberal culture, quite the opposite tendency is most operative, at any rate in the field of religious controversy.

We have noted already that our civilization has accepted the "mana" of Christianity, while increasingly rebelling against its implications. Few contemporary non-believers would willingly proclaim themselves un-Christian. They will claim as a rule for their different moral codes or social manners the sanction of what they call the "Christian Ethic"; their emphasis is on likeness not on difference, the desire to minimize religious cleavage. To some extent we can see in such a tendency merely the transference of our interest from religious to purely political allegiance; it is very largely for this reason that in England the religious issue itself is so obscured, but yet I believe it would not have been possible so to obscure the fundamental issue if we had not first already so far confused it through loose thinking and loose usage of our words.

The general principle of such a movement is familiar to us in the current phrase of a "United Front" against Fascism or against Communism, as the case may be. It does not matter greatly which Front we take for our purpose, in both the essential emphasis is the same:

"Let us leave aside our minor differences; in the face of far more vital, serious questions, we cannot afford to waste our time on trifles. Let us unite on the important issues on which we are all agreed, on the forms of temporal government we desire, on our national interests, on the balance of power. Opinions and theological speculation are luxuries that we cannot now indulge in; we can, if we wish, enjoy them at our leisure when the really important matters have been settled."

This is in principle the agreed position of either form of United-Front allegiance; temporal and spiritual values are reversed. It is part of the process we have been observing: the reversal of the natural order of value which follows from the original self-assertion, the contracting universe, the mechanization of life.

Yet though we can see this process as one process, following through its various manifestations, as it should logically follow its beginning, we should do well to study each example, so far as it is possible to do so. In this particular United Front to-day, particular aspects of the movement strike one.

The first thing, and perhaps the most important, is the complete and genuine misunderstanding of what the religious view itself implies. The Pagan as such is unable to understand why the Christian as such cannot share his point of view. He looks on the Christian's refusal to join with him as arbitrary and unreasonable and discourteous. "He could help me if he liked and he will not help," is the general reaction to the refusal; often he will describe it as "un-Christian."

We have already touched upon the difficulty there is in defining the true meaning of the word "Christian"; we have defined it as signifying in essence a belief in the supernatural order of being, transcending and outweighing the world of sense, a Theocentric orientation of life, but the part which such a belief does in practice play in the total *Weltanschauung* of different people varies as much as individual faces.

We have, at one end, the Totalitarian Christian, to whom this faith in God is his whole life, a reality blotting out and obscuring all other interests; he is, in this pure form, extremely rare, but between him and the vaguest, most diluted Christian we find every degree of half-belief and corresponding devotion to such belief.

It is theoretically possible to hold a complete belief with indifference, to affirm half-hearted allegiance to some cause which in itself demands complete devotion, but it is almost impossible to imagine a wholehearted devotion to half-hearted faith. We are then justified in the generalization that, as a rule, the more definite and more complete the faith, the more totalitarian will be the devotion to it.

Whatever faith we profess, it is probable, we being imperfect mortals and not saints, that our practice will lag very far behind our profession. We do not become heroic and un-selfish by the mere fact of knowing we should be so, but, admitting this, we still can, and do, assert that the idea which we set before us, the Truth we affirm and acknowledge, does affect our whole mental calibre and our conduct to a larger extent than any other factor. A faith which demands our absolute allegiance will obtain a larger measure of devotion than the half-hearted, watered-down "opinion." We see this illustrated in the case before us, the response to the challenge of the "United Front."

The average intermediate Christian, so confronted, must choose between the two sides of himself, the rationalistic, common sense, social being, and the uncertain, on-the-defensive Christian; we see in how many cases the first pre-vails. He accepts, in fact, the position suggested to him, that belief in God is of secondary importance compared to more urgent material advantage.

The intransigent attitude of Catholic Christians towards co-operation with anti-religious bodies of any kind has been a serious cause of misunderstanding, almost, one might say, a cause of scandal, and because it is illustrative of so much besides, I think we should do well to pursue it further.

We are not concerned here with political issues, nor with either form of existing United Front; it is clear that, whichever standpoint is adopted, it is for political ends and advantages that it is formed, and as such neither has interest for us here; Hitler is no more Christian than is Stalin; but, as often in political questions, we can see a reflection of moral and mental conflicts, so here, in these movements for the United Front, we have illustrations of a tendency and a wish which is active and spreading in quite other spheres.

In the religious field we see the same impulse more articulate, in the recent Summer School of Protestant Churches at Oxford, and the movements towards re-union between Anglicans and Non-conformists of different kinds. Much of this is surely good and should be welcomed; there are clearly cases where difference of opinion is trivial or without significance, where only pride or obstinacy keeps apart bodies of people who belong together; but, allowing for all this, our more immediate danger would seem to be the desire for unity at the expense of truth.

We are still left with our essential difference, between the Good Pagan outlook and the Christian.

It will be objected here that many Christians are on the other side in the question under discussion, that we are claiming for one type of Christian a monopoly to which he has no right. It is true that we do take here the Catholic Christian standpoint as the true Christian type, and we do so because it is the most complete antithesis to what we have called the Good Pagan position, to what he himself prefers to call "Rationalist."

There are countless ways of dividing up the world, from

good and bad, black and white, rich and poor, endlessly, but in this particular context our division must be between the religious and non-religious, what we have so far called the Christian and the Good Pagan. We have already considered these two types and defined the Christian, for our classification as the man dependent on the supernatural, and the Pagan as one who rejects it; we have admitted repeatedly that there are in practice innumerable variations on and combinations between these two positions; but if this definition is in its essence the true one, we are justified in taking Catholicism as the most complete type of the religious outlook as opposed to the Good Pagan or Freethinker.

The essence of Catholic Christianity is acceptance of a Supernatural Order, here and now, at every point and turn of daily life, impinging as it were on all we do, breaking through, always at hand, always real; the essence of the Rationalist Good Pagan is denial of such a Supernatural Order, anywhere, altogether. The varieties of intermediate belief are all attempts at compromise between them; the numberless different forms of Protestantism are all, if we attempt to analyse them, but bits of Catholic faith taken from their context, mixed up with different proportions of rationalism. The recently published report on Anglican doctrine provides in itself clear illustration of this; outside the indeterminate ranks of Anglicanism we find a still wider range of disbelief still claiming for itself the Christian sanction. We may find corroboration of our assertion in the differing degrees of hostility shown by the avowedly anti-religious towards the different forms of Christian thought; active hostility is reserved almost entirely for the Catholic Christians, the others are neglected as unimportant or in some cases accepted as half-allies.

In the main, however, what we are concerned with is less hostility than misunderstanding. Hostility does exist, we cannot deny it, in some countries it has reached acute persecution, but that is a clear and straightforward situation, it is as old as the Church; the problem we are pursuing in these pages is more puzzling, and more insidious and more widespread. Leaving aside all hostile opposition, we are still confronted with an almost overpowering weight of misunderstanding on the part of a world that believes itself to be friendly, that claims for itself our ideas and our name. This confusion of the issue is in the long run more dangerous than active opposition; it deprives us, before we see what has been happening, even of the means to defend ourselves. If we are not on our guard and on the alert, we may hear the cock crowing, we may find that, without knowing what we did, we denied Christ.[1]

II

In considering this question of the United Front, one of the principal obstacles has been, and still is, the use of the term Christian to cover so very many quite different ideas. We have already touched on this difficulty in our earlier consideration of the Good Pagan, but in relation to the United Front we must examine it from another angle; the contrasting forms of so-called Christian opinion involve us in continual misunderstandings.

We have an example of such confusion in recent pronounce-

---

[1] Cf., *The Times*, Monday, May 2nd, 1938.
   "The forces positively opposed to Christianity are smaller, probably, in this country than anywhere else in the world. Hostility is negligible, by comparison with indifference; but whereas hostility hammers, indifference rusts, and the latter may be the quicker cause of the metal giving way under strain."

ments of the Dean of Canterbury, when he describes Soviet Russia or Red Spain as "truly Christian," and finds in revolutionary anti-religious outbreaks no evidence of anti-Christian feeling.

The Dean has given offence in many quarters by statements of this kind, but I think it is easy to understand his meaning, and to a certain extent to sympathize.

What he means to say is, presumably, that, in spite of being anti-religious, these people are inexplicably "good"; he finds them sincere, self-sacrificing, brave; he finds in them qualities which are expected of Christians, and which Christians do not in every case possess. That this should be so, is striking, perhaps upsetting; it attracts our notice rightly, if true, and it may be true; the Dean has done well to draw our attention to it, but what he has said is in fact something quite different; he uses his words wrongly through confusion of ideas.

To be "good" is not the same as to be Christian, although being Christian should include being "good".

This leads us on to more controversial questions as to what goodness is, and how far we are agreed; that is a point that we must consider later; for the moment we must assume some large measure of agreement in the ordinary virtues that we admire, what we may call perhaps the "natural virtues"; but to claim for Christians a monopoly of them is surely more intolerant and exclusive than the Dean of Canterbury could wish to be.

One consequence of this loose use of words is a watering-down of the whole force and power of the Christian impact against, or perhaps towards, the Pagan world.

I myself once heard a distinguished Anglican preacher describe Christianity as very easy, simply being a little kinder and more patient to "an aunt you do not like," and so on.

Now we should all agree that a good Christian should be kind to people in general, aunts included, but a view of life which holds such kindness to be the sole, or indeed the chief, character of Christianity is very far removed from the totalitarian view. True kindness is a valuable virtue, but we may doubt if the high premium set upon that one virtue to-day is a sign that we should welcome. Very often "kindness" is used when "indifference" would be truer; not to blame, not to condemn, not to "take a strong line about," all this is understood by being kind; how often, in fact, is what is classed as kindness, merely a shirking of responsibility? "Live and let live" is the popular attitude, it is pleasant, and it is easy, but it is not either truly kind, or Christian, nor is any kindness that can be described as easy.

Christianity is not easy, it is difficult; its appeal is not and cannot be to those who demand a comfortable life; it is a challenge, not a soporific.

To present it in such diluted, distorted form can surely lead us nowhere; it means nothing. How can such a view be reconciled with such texts as:

"Strait is the way and narrow is the gate, and few there be that find it."

"If any man will follow Me, let him take up his cross, and follow Me"?

and countless others which proclaim explicitly, the austere and formidable and totalitarian nature of the Christian life.

This diluted "Christianity without tears" does, it is true, disarm opposition; you cannot feel much hostility to a jelly, nor to an eiderdown. It is impossible to have anti-clerical outbreaks against so negative a protagonist, but is to escape notice all we aim at?

In opposition to totalitarianism, appeal is often made to

the early Christians as examples of this "simple kindness" view, but, as Mr. Belloc has pointed out, this vague kindliness would never have provoked the persecutions to which the early Christians were subjected. Diocletian and Nero knew what they were about; just as Hitler and Stalin know in our own day. These persecutors are justified from their point of view; they recognize the existence at their doors of an irreconcilable, totalitarian force, whose existence is in itself a challenge to them.

In order to clarify a little further the incompatibility between these two views of what is Christian, it will be best to give illustrations from recognized leaders of both schools of thought.

We have quoted "being kinder to one's aunt" as an example of the "without tears" presentment, also some statements of the Dean of Canterbury, but these may be thought unrepresentative; there are quite other versions of dilution; we will therefore give two extracts more at length from two acknowledged leaders of such opinion, in both of which we see from different angles the process of displacing God by Man. The first is from the Bishop of Birmingham's well-known book, *Should such a Faith Offend?*

> "Not only do I think that we may conclude that (such) a generalized religious outlook, if I may so term it, is indestructible, but, as it seems to me, we have solid ground for believing that the Christian faith will continue to be a persuasive inspiration to humanity. . . . Christianity, in so far as it is true to its founder, remains psychologically sound. Speaking for myself then, I say boldly that religion is not only a most necessary, but also an indestructible element in man's heritage. . . .
>
> "Man is a product of Nature, an emergent in the Divine Scheme. Civilized man is the highest emergent

of which we have knowledge. I take it, then, that in him we see, at the highest level we can reach, the end to which the unity behind Nature is tending. If we denote this unity behind Nature by God, we find God's purpose most fully displayed in the evolution of civilized Man. The qualities which in our civilization we are perforce developing and finding increasingly valuable, are those which God has desired to bring into existence. They are the clearest indications we can get of His Nature.".

The second extract is from Dean Inge's *Faith and Knowledge.*

"The solidarity of the human race, and even of all living things, seems to me to be the great truth which has become more vivid to us in the last fifty years. It is affecting our opinions, religious, moral and social, in many ways. It has broken down the old dualism of natural and supernatural, teaching us to find natural law in the spiritual world and spiritual in the natural; it has changed our feelings about the lower animals, so that the cruelties of sport and fashion are as surely doomed to moral reprobation as were the shows of the amphitheatre 1,800 years ago; it has given us a new sense of our duty towards posterity, involving moral responsibility in matters which in former times were seldom considered as right and wrong; it has (in conjugation with other causes), evolved a new sensitiveness to the infliction of needless suffering; it has exalted our conception of the world we live in, which, instead of a place of exile and trial, is now regarded as the predestined scene of the Civitas Dei, the perfected human society wherein God's will may be done on earth as it is in Heaven; it has dignified and even consecrated all the nobler human activities which are capable of forming a part of that higher civilization; it has made us impatient of seeing any class or individual excluded from the privilege of contributing to this work, and of sharing in what has been already gained. It is, in a sense, a new morality, inasmuch as the emphasis of praise and blame is being modified in many particulars."

I think that these two extracts, in addition to those already quoted, do give us a very fair idea of diluted Christianity, the sincere attempt to effect a compromise between the Rationalist and religious views, a bridge between the Pagan and the Christian. In order to show how far such compromise has led us from the totalitarian position, we will now give two totalitarian extracts:

The famous prayer of St. Ignatius sums it up most completely:

"Take and receive, Oh Lord, my entire liberty,
My memory, my understanding, my whole will;
All that I am or possess is from Thee;
To Thee, do I give them back, to do with according to
　　Thy pleasure.
Give me only love of Thee, and Thy grace, and I am
　　rich enough,
Nor do I ask for anything beside."

This is in itself perhaps enough to illustrate the alternative attitude, but in case some more modern example should be preferred in opposition to the modern Bishop and Dean, we may give the following passage from Cardinal Newman:

"Why is the framework of civilized society all so graceful and correct? Why, on the other hand, is there so much of emotion, so much of conflicting and alternating feeling, so much that is high, so much that is debased in the devotion of Christianity? It is because the Christian, and the Christian alone, has a revelation of God; it is because he has upon his mind, in his heart, in his conscience, the idea of One who is self-dependent, who is from Everlasting, who is Incommunicable. He knows that One alone is holy, and that His own creatures are so frail in comparison of Him that they would dwindle and melt away in His presence, did He not uphold them by His power. He knows that there is One whose greatness and whose blessedness are not affected, the centre of whose stability is not moved, by the presence or absence of the whole creation with its innumerable beings and portions; whom nothing can touch, nothing can increase or diminish, who was as mighty before He made the worlds as since, and as serene and blissful since He made them as before. He knows that there is just One being in whose hand lies his own happiness, his own sanctity, his own life and hope and salvation. He knows that there is One to whom he owes everything, and against whom he can have no plea or remedy. 'All things are nothing before Him; the highest things do but worship Him the more, the holiest beings are such, only because they have a greater portion of Him. . . .

"This then, my brethren, is the reason why every son of man, whatever his degree of holiness, whether a returning prodigal, or a matured saint, says with the Publican: 'Oh, God, be merciful to me'; it is because created natures high and low are all on a level in the sight and in comparison of the Creator and so all of them have one speech and one only, whether it be the thief on the cross, Magdalen at the feast, or St. Paul before his martyrdom; not that one of them may not have what another has not, but one and all have nothing but what comes from Him, and are as nothing before Him who is all in all."[1]

I think we can recognize from these two sets of quotations that the ideas presented to us are quite different; the whole conception of man's relation to life, to the world, to God, is different. We can see that the first contains but a fractional part of what is in the second, mixed with so large a proportion

[1] Newman. *Sermons Preached on Various Occasions*, 25–9.

of Good Pagan moderation that the final result is far more near to that.

It would be interesting to trace historically the rise of the modern humanitarian Christianity; that it is modern and new, as it claims to be, there can be no doubt. The most superficial acquaintance with the old Puritans would dispel any hope of meeting with it there, nor do we find it in George Fox the first Quaker, nor in Wesley; it is not then intrinsic to Protestantism as such, though it may prove to be its logical outcome. We may take it, in fact, to be but the latest of many different attempts at dilution, the watering-down of a drink that is too strong, a weakening of the medicine that is too nasty.

One significant sign of this latest tendency is the dislike among many good pro-Christians of the Crucifix, or even of pictures of the Crucifixion. This has nothing whatever to do with Puritanism or disapproval of images or pictures. "It is too sad," "I don't like to think about it!" are typical expressions of this feeling.

III

In dealing with this "dilutionism" as our opponent, we are not forgetting the continued existence, in many quarters, of real and militant anti-religious feeling; that this continues always underneath the various forms of united front advances, the world situation leaves no room for doubt.

The two outlooks, the two loyalties, are in their essence hostile, they are mutually exclusive and destructive, and the underlying antagonism is liable to break through in any time of stress or of upheaval. That it may do so here at any time we are aware, it is indeed essential to our position that there is and must be this intrinsic opposition between the two points of view that we describe. We are not neglecting or denying this when we cite, as an example of misconception, the conciliatory dilutionist approach. Its very wish to approach and conciliate us illustrates in itself the misunderstanding which may be more dangerous than opposition. We have shown in earlier pages how distorted was the deliberately hostile picture of our position; in the conciliatory attitude we find from a different angle an unconscious distortion that is comparable.

From different points, and with different intention, we meet with similar misrepresentation.

It would obviously be a *reductio ad absurdum* to say that there was more hope of understanding between the militant atheist and the Christian than between the totalitarian Christian and mild agnostic, but it would be true to say that in the militant atheist, in spite of the misrepresentations we have dealt with, there is, fundamental in his militancy, a recognition of the supreme importance of the questions under discussion, and in this he agrees with the totalitarian Christian; they are both in this sense at least religious-minded, they are dealing, to that extent, in the same medium, whereas in the dilutionist, united-front attitude this question, which to both of them is vital, is relegated to a secondary position, or even ruled out altogether from our attention.

The examples which we have cited in this connection have been so far from professedly Christian sources, who are themselves approaching Paganism, whose avowed intention is to bring Christianity into a form acceptable to the Pagan; they take the initiative in the compromise, but what is more significant and important is *rapprochement* from the other side, the wish on the part of moderate Good Pagans to make their terms with Christianity. It might seem, at first, that agreement should be easy with such good will apparent from both

sides, yet it is notable that there is little progress. The diluted
modernist Christianity offered is unsatisfactory to the earnest
Pagan, it is too weak, too insipid, too unreal; it is the totalitarian that attracts him, yet he finds himself, at the same time,
repelled.

The totalitarian quality of Catholicism is one of the principal
stumbling blocks to-day in the way of understanding from
outside, yet it is at the same time its great attraction.

Now in especial, in these post-war years of trouble and
disillusionment and chaos, there is discernible on every side, in
the Good Pagan world of which we speak, a questioning of
the truth of unbelief. The dogmatic rationalism of our fathers
is in its turn being questioned and disbelieved. One cannot
even be sure that God is not, nor positive, as one was, that
religious values are nonsense. Anyone who is known to have
been a convert from this same Pagan world will be astonished
at the people from it who ask him questions, half shamefacedly,
about his unaccountable point of view. From absolutely
unsuspected quarters he will be asked what it is like to be a
Christian, and as a rule the first question is, "Are you happy?"

That there is a great body of such people, fumbling and
questioning, wanting "to be happy," dissatisfied with the ideals
put before them, the God-substitutes on which they have
been taught to depend, of this there can be no doubt.

These people are attracted by what seems to them spiritual
and permanent in contrast to the tumultuous, short-distance
rhythm of life; they enjoy the peace and dignity of churches,
they admire the moral stand of Catholics, sometimes they
have been interested in saints, but, almost always, they shrink
and are rebuffed when they meet, in whatever form it may
confront them, the totalitarian element in religion.

They say in fact:

"Can we not join together? In the face of such grave dangers to all good living as we are faced with now, the old quarrels and points of difference should be dropped; there is so much we appreciate in religion, especially in real religion like yours; it may even be true, or partly true, it may, still more probably, be necessary to humanity in some form or other: we believe it is, and we like your form so much better than the others. Let us share with you the strength and peace you have, that at least we think you have—only we must still be free to differ from you, to take or leave the different things we want."

This is in the spiritual and mental sphere, the counterpart of the United Front in politics.

And the answer they receive seems a rebuff:

"You cannot have something for nothing; you cannot have your cake and eat it; you must lose your soul to save it . . ." and so on endlessly; in endlessly different forms, they are met with the same answer. It is, if we view it from another angle, the old story of the young ruler with great possessions. If you are not prepared to give, you will not receive, and the giving required here is totalitarian.

It is not merely a sense of personal rebuff with which we have to deal, it is a more general and more serious revulsion, almost one might call it moral indignation, at what, to the inquirer, seems narrow-mindedness, and unkindness, and the usual indictment which we have to meet is the familiar one of being un-Christian.

IV

If we are to try and justify or explain this apparent intolerance, this totalitarianism, we must present it somehow in our accuser's language; we must try, if we can, to see it through his eyes, to explain it, if we are able, in the terms he uses.

From this point of view, all appeals to authority or legal technicalities are useless; he accepts no authority outside his private judgment; it is to him incredible that anyone else should honestly accept it.

The position in his eyes is quite arbitrary; we shut him out because we do not want him, we decide, again quite arbitrarily, that we are right and he is wrong, when any reasonable being recognizes that neither of us can be in the least certain; we each have our own opinion, that is all.

What we must endeavour to explain is that this very exclusiveness and certainty is in itself the essence of our "opinion." When he asserts as final that "no one knows," that "everything is subjective supposition," he is asserting as certain his own Agnostic Dogma, he is being in fact every bit as dogmatic as we are.

He must realize that, however strange he thinks it, the essential belief on which we base our faith is that truth is real and objective, and independent of our views about it, and that it is therefore both illogical and impossible for us to accept the proposition he makes us, which is the negation of our whole position.

We shall find that a large measure of our difficulty in understanding each other's point of view lies in this question of subjectivism. We shall find that the concept of "objective truth" is incomprehensible to the modern agnostic; he will say that he appreciates our position and only wants us to be reasonable, but the fact is that he does not understand in the least what it is. He feels convinced throughout that we are able to modify what we hold at our own will, just as he knows he can, with his beliefs.

He may of course be right; it may be an illusion on our part that for us the case is different, but in that case it is this precise illusion with which he has to deal. It is the very essence of our belief, or our illusion, if he prefers that name, that there is an actual body of known truth; that there is the whole difference between being and not being, between what is true and what is not; it is our belief, or illusion, that we know this; we are assured that what we know has an objective reality of its own, that our belief does not give it existence, our ceasing to believe would not affect it.

When we are asked to compromise about it, it is as though we were asked to bear false witness in order to oblige a friend in trouble, in order to show our friendliness or good will; if we refuse, we are blamed as un-Christian.

"I would do the same for you," our neighbour says, "why should you make so much fuss about a trifle? and perhaps, after all, you may have been mistaken in what you thought you saw or heard or did?"

For almost everybody there is, if we can find it, some absolute value somewhere, to which he holds; it may be some matter of quite personal conduct, never to tell a lie, or betray a friend, or be a coward, or it may be some quite abstract generalization, such as that we know, and can know, nothing, but even such complete scepticism implies in itself a loyalty to truth; why should the Logical Positivist take trouble to proclaim his disbelief except from devotion to what he thinks true? This allegiance to the truth, as best we see it, is the strongest common ground on which to build.

Few of the most extreme subjectivists would deny that to follow what we think the truth, is good; can we not, then, get them to understand that what we think, subjectively if they like, is that our truth is not in fact subjective?

We may like it or not like it, may wish it different, but it remains the truth, and we cannot change it to suit our needs or those of other people; if this is what we think, however wrongly, surely they must agree that we should act upon it.

In current life we do all assume some impressions to be objective, others as subject to our own emotions, and this on whichever side our allegiance lies; but to carry this classification on to the abstract plane, into what we are taught to call "ideology," brings us to a new divergence. The recognition of objective truth implies acceptance of existing things as independent of our personal will, the subjective attitude, on the other hand, lays ever-increasing emphasis on ourselves. If things are so, because we feel them so, we are in fact the arbiters of life.

The totalitarian attitude altogether is characterized by acceptance as the principle of our attitude to life, the Pagan or Agnostic by rejection, for the sake of personal choice and independence; it is in essence, as we suggested earlier, the expression of self-assertion and aggression in our attitude to the universe around us.

We are reminded of the lady who announced to Thomas Carlyle:

"Mr. Carlyle, I accept the universe!" And his answer:

"Egad, Madam, you'd better!"

Put against this we have the lines of Henley:

> "I am the master of my fate,
> I am the Captain of my soul!"

He does not accept the universe, he defies it, and these lines express very plainly the sentiment which is at the back of the revulsion against totalitarian religion, it is the extreme assertion of independence, which permeates so many forms of thought to-day.

The description of God as an Oriental Potentate, with which we are all familiar, is but another version of the Old Man in the sky, but it is more enlightening as to the motives behind it. The attitude of acceptance characteristic of all forms of totalitarian religion is felt to be servile, to be dependent even upon God is found degrading.

Absolute dependence upon God and upon God's will is the prime sign of totalitarianism, and it is precisely this factor in it which is hardest to explain acceptably to the average well-intentioned English mind;[1] other aspects may be more noticed in other countries.

The mental atmosphere of English public opinion is far more decided and formative a force than most of us are inclined to recognize. We are told from our earliest days, and we believe it, that in England thought is free from propaganda, that there is no pressure to conformity in a free democratic culture like our own. There are, we are told, merely a few quite general principles upon which we are all agreed; to question these would be to be un-English, a very strong and decisive condemnation, but no one, to speak of, dreams of questioning them.

Now these principles which we know as "Democratic" are, if we examine them, all of one essential stock, all forms of self-assertive independence, the various forms of self-determina-

---

[1] "It is one great peculiarity of the Christian character to be dependent. Men of the world indeed, in proportion as they are active and enterprising, boast of their independence, and are proud of having obligations to no one, but it is the Christian's excellence ... to be willing to serve, and to rejoice in the permission to do so, to be content to view himself in a subordinate position."
Newman, *Parochial and Plain Sermons* vii, 251-2.

tion and self-government on which, politically, we pride
ourselves.

It is not our purpose to discuss political democracy, and its
defects or its advantages, we are only concerned with the influence of these political forms and ideas, as we are accustomed to
them in the mental and spiritual attitude around us. In England
we are so much identified with our own political institutions
that we do, without realizing it, constantly carry over these
rather special political theories into quite other departments of
our life and thought. We do attach to our political theories an
almost sacred infallibility. The system on which we base our
political structure is endowed for us with Divine authority,
it becomes a necessary basis of moral judgment, and this we
carry into our private life and our relations towards life and
death and God.

This means in practice a strong tendency to demand a
Constitutional Democratic God who will co-operate with us
on equal terms.

Anyone who has read the religious articles which appear
frequently in the Sunday papers will be familiar with phrases
such as: "My God must be . . .", "I cannot accept a God
who . . ." etc.

These articles, written for the most part by personalities
of the stage or screen or sport, are characteristic, in this attitude, of a far more serious and distinguished public. We have
an example of the highest kind in Mr. Lionel Curtis's "Civitas
Dei"; is not the choice of title in itself suggestive? Mr. Curtis
finds that the idea of God is useful for the well-being of the
British Commonwealth, but a God whose chief function is to
be of use to a free Commonwealth of self-governing nations
must, it is clear, conform constitutionally; he must be freely
elected, and representative, limited strictly in His functions

and powers, the servant and not the master of the supreme Commonwealth. This idea, which to any totalitarian Christian seems so ludicrous as to obliterate blasphemy, has been welcomed with respect and approbation by most serious organs of British public opinion. It expresses, only in a more articulate form, the average good Englishman's "God-reaction."

What we must understand in this connection is that this demand for a Constitutional God is not by such minds regarded as a weakness to be deprecated or excused in any way, it is thought of as a rational adaptation of the old religious theories to modern needs, it is approved and given moral sanction. If we place in opposition to this idea the totalitarian cry of Job: "Although He should kill me, I will trust in Him!" we have in a nutshell the antithesis of our outlooks.

We start from two opposing standpoints, so far antagonistic that it seems, at times, quite hopeless to reach any common understanding. In the one case our premise is human welfare as expressed, for Englishmen, politically; certain principles of self-determination and humanity are assumed as certain good, this we know; everything else is indefinite and uncertain. If some religious belief can be harmonized to fit in with this dogma, we will admit it, but not otherwise. The Kingdom of Heaven must be transformable into the Representative Parliament of Heaven; if it cannot be so transformed, we must liquidate it.

In opposition to this, on the other side, we start from belief in an Almighty God as the one supreme and all-important truth, and the Will of God as the one certain good. Human institutions of all kinds, human welfare as we imagine it, are all subservient to, contingent on, it.

From such a point of view we are not sure that the British Constitution is more exactly suited to God's will than many entirely alien constitutions; we may hope it is, we may even try to make it so conform as best we can, but, were there any clear conflict between them, there is no doubt where our allegiance lies.

This ultimate allegiance is clearly recognized in the present crisis between Nazi Germany and the Church; here again we see illustrated, in the external and political field, a problem which is universal and individual also.

Having given these semi-political examples, let us go back to our individual case of the well-wishing inquirer who is rebuffed personally, and outraged morally, by the exclusive aspect of Totalitarianism.

We have tried to explain to him that it is the same love of truth, which he himself affirms, that obliges us in our turn to reject his offers. He faces us always, in essentials, with the same protest: "I am quite ready to admit that you may be right, if you, on your side, will admit the same for me; there must be give and take, and compromise."

V

Now, apart from the prime question of what is true, and the recognized obligation on us all to stick to the truth as we see it, and to nothing else, there is here another consideration. The Good Pagan who approaches us in this way is clearly assuming that there is some advantage to be won by his proposal; what is it that he is hoping to obtain by his approach to us? What is he offering to give us in return? This is a fundamental question, for if we could convince him on this point, we should have gone far to clear the way between us.

That the kind of advance we have suggested here is in some form or other very general, we have only to glance at recent books to see; there have been a flood of such wooings of religion in post-war years, from Mr. Wells's *God the Invisible King*, through Mr. Middleton Murry's book *God*, Mr. Joad, Mr. Heard, Mr. Curtis, Mr. Julian Huxley, and now, most lately, Mr. Aldous Huxley.

It is not our intention to examine here the differences in these various attempts to reconcile free Paganism with God. Much of this writing has been interesting, both in itself and still more from the sociological point of view, but in all we can see two persisting and opposing trends, however disguised and excused, or explained away.

The first and most important is, of course, that all these rational scientific Pagans are in their different ways, and from different angles, dissatisfied with the purely material outlook, the purely mechanical Godless Universe which they have been instrumental in building up. They are all men whose opinions influence others, and as there is in practice constant interplay in such matters between leaders and led, we may assume that the doubt and dissatisfaction of these leaders implies a similar doubt and similar dissatisfaction throughout the literary and scientific circles they represent. They are conscious that something is lacking in their world, that there is something which they have not got, which they suspect is possessed by other people. This aspect of the case is very important, for, in the current hierarchy of values, "to be happy" is the most widely accepted as valid, even the respect for truth, which we have claimed as still generally operative, gives way, under any stress, to this test of happiness. It is even made the arbiter of truth: "If it makes me happy, it is true for me." "You cannot know what is right or wrong, you can know what makes you happy or unhappy," and so on.

These leaders of contemporary thought, as the writers we

have referred to would be styled, have found in practice that they are not happy, nor are their friends, nor their followers and disciples. They find that, having repudiated all the obvious barriers to happiness, having taken where they could and what they could, having broken the old restricting prohibitions and seized upon the maximum of freedom, they are less happy than their fathers were who were still bound by much restricting habit.

To many such people, a believing Christian in actual life is probably unknown, the segregation of circles is so great, but they are readers and their lives are largely lived in books; others, more fortunate, chance to meet a Christian, by which we mean, of course, a Totalitarian Christian. What strikes them in the first place is not "goodness," that is a value about which they are not sure, but they notice, generally, that he seems "happy," that is at least how they would themselves express it; from that their interest leads them on to ask how in a reasonable universe happiness can arise from being foolish. There is a cynical retort that says "Only the fool is happy in the world as it is!" but these minds that we are considering go further, that answer is inadequate for them. They argue: "This man who holds erroneous beliefs, who has subjected both his thought and his action to ridiculous and obnoxious restrictions, has in despite of that got hold of something real, which we, in all our wisdom, have not got."

And from that standpoint all these books are written.

All these writers may go further, the books we have referred to may be followed by others, some or all may be but first steps in a progression; but, judging them as they are, as expressions of a general frame of mind which is far more widespread than the immediate public of any of the individual writers named, we can recognize in them all the same false value, all of them assume the Anthropocentric standpoint, almost, one might say, the Egocentric, and all are attempts to get something for nothing, short cuts to beatitude, of different kinds.

We have seen how Mr. Curtis, in the political field, allows his constitutional God a minor part; we can see in Mr. Aldous Huxley's work the same attitude in the psychological. Mr. Huxley's interests are more spiritual; he is concerned with the soul and the soul's needs. He is prepared to admit that he has been wrong in certain views he used to hold before, but only a very little wrong in a few views. What he is in fact concerned with in this book is to persuade his readers, and, I think, himself, that it is possible to obtain the advantage which he admits the religious man to possess, without incurring the disabilities which up till now have been associated with them. For this purpose he deals largely with the most extreme and purest form of religious man, the mystic.

In taking St. John of the Cross as his type of religious mind, few would quarrel with him, but his attitude to that great saint seems strangely arrogant and presumptuous; it might almost be summed up in the old condemnation that "this silly fellow doesn't even know his own silly business!"

Now it is quite a possible line of argument to say that St. John of the Cross's way of life was silly, or at least mistaken or useless; according to certain standards of value, no doubt it was, but Mr. Huxley does not take that line. His argument would seem to be as follows: "There is such a thing as mystical experience; it is a good thing; it has been supposed, by those who indulged in it, to imply a belief in a God of a more or less definite and personal nature; the Mystics supposed, because they were unenlightened, that their experiences were in fact contact with such a God, and proof of His existence, but I know better. I can show you how to attain the happiness which St. John of the Cross attained without the very unpleasant preliminaries which he thought necessary, and without the very repellent superstition on which he supposed his experiences to depend."

Now, to any of us who are able to share, at least, the beliefs of St. John of the Cross, it seems both presumptuous to a high degree, and also extraordinarily stupid, to write so.

To deal with so totalitarian a believer as St. John of the Cross, to admire him, to profess a wish to attain what he attained, but without the faith which was his entire being, leaves us wondering what Mr. Huxley in fact admires him for. It is as though one professed to admire a blue sky without the blueness, fire without light or heat, water without wetness, or anything else deprived of the very quality which it is.

St. John of the Cross himself says:

> "And by this means alone, that is Faith, God manifests Himself to the soul in the Divine Light which surpasseth all understanding, and, therefore, the greater the Faith of the soul, the more is it united to God."[1]

And again:

> "What the soul tastes now in this touch of God, is in truth, though not perfectly, a certain foretaste of everlasting life. It is not incredible, when we believe, as we do believe, that this touch is most substantial, and that the substance of God touches the substance of the soul."[2]

Does Mr. Huxley really know more about it?

St. John of the Cross, deprived of faith, would remain an undifferentiated sixteenth-century Spaniard of no particular significance at all.

[1] *Mount Carmel*, Bk. II, 9. I.   [2] *Living Flame*, Stan. II, 22.

The secret of this nonsense, for it is nonsense, is not in truth a matter of stupidity at all, it lies in a moral and emotional failure; the refusal to admit oneself wrong and the foolish, right; the shrinking from giving in, giving up, surrender, which one tries to justify by appeal to reason.[1]

VI

It is not only the dogmatic faith from which Mr. Huxley and his friends recoil; it is the whole Theocentric view of life, and the reversal of value that this implies; how great that reversal is, it is hard to face nor even understand when one has faced it. To those who have been brought up at all as Christians, such revaluation must be, at least verbally, familiar, but, for all that, it may be unrealized; to those who come upon it as new, in adult life, the shock and newness are almost overpowering.

All the old values have to be discarded; gradually, bit by bit, it becomes apparent how much there is to discard, not only what is wrong intrinsically, for that would be no new idea to the Good Pagan, but what in itself is good, for what is better; ways of approach, and motives and lines of judgment, what is to be considered and what ignored.

"First things shall be last and last, first," is true here as it is in other contexts; most painfully and slowly, we apprehend it, but without this apprehension we get nowhere.

[1] Cf., Newman, *Parochial and Plain Sermons* v, 241–2.
"When a man comes to God to be saved, then I say the essence of true conversion is surrender of himself, an unreserved unconditional surrender, and this is a saying which most men who come to God cannot receive; they wish to be saved, but in their own way. They wish, as it were, to capitulate, but upon terms, to carry off their goods with them."

The expression, "a good humbling experience," is in itself an illustration of this reversal of values in current practice, not applied, as it might be by the Good Pagan, to someone who is *hubristic* or conceited, but simply a quite matter-of-fact acceptance of what is unpleasant or painful as to be welcomed, not to be put up with, be it noted, but to be welcomed, to be pleased with, to be happy about.

This reversal of value must be understood as something completely unlike Puritanism; with that attitude of mind we are familiar in whatever religious belief we have been brought up. The Puritan turn of mind has become temperamental in certain types of English character, quite apart from any theological tenets, and its supposed connection with religion has done a great deal of harm.

Religion has been so much identified with this negative, repressive, joyless attitude that any suggestion of asceticism is very readily misunderstood.

The whole essence of the reversal of value is opposed to this, it is positive joy in what, by nature, we should have disenjoyed, because we suffer for the Love of God, because our suffering is one with Christ's. The end, and not the means, is all important. It is not that we like to be unhappy, or humiliated, or outcast as an end in itself, but because the demand of God, the Love of God, is so totalitarian in its nature that there is no room for anything besides, and even suffering or ignominy can be, in relation to God, perfect joy.

One of the most perfect expressions of this position is St. Francis of Assisi's famous discourse to Brother Leo on Perfect Joy, which ends:

> "Above all gifts and graces of the Holy Spirit which God our Master granteth to those that love Him, is to overcome oneself, and willingly for the Love of God to

undergo pains and privations and hardships and tribulations."[1]

The same idea is expressed by St. John of the Cross:

> "But to seek God in Himself is not only to be willingly deprived of this thing or that for God, but to incline ourselves to will and choose for Christ's sake whatever is most disagreeable, whether proceeding from God or from the world. This is to love God."[2]

Or by St. Paul:

> "Therefore I take pleasure in infirmities, in reproaches, in necessities, in persecutions, in distresses, for Christ; for when I am weak, then am I strong."[3]

Or from a more modern writer:

> "We learn then that in the conflict of His standard and our own, loss may be gain, and frustration fulfilment, and death life."[4]

Pages of quotations from spiritual writers could be quoted to illustrate this truth if it were needed; it is the necessity of the Cross in Christianity; to the believing Christian, a foregone conclusion, to the convert, a staggering revelation, to the tentative inquirer, a stumbling block that is, too often, final.

We do not mean to suggest that believing Christians do in effect all attain to such a state; it is only too obvious that very few attain it; but the goal at which we aim, the ideas we live by, do make an enormous difference to our lives; it is, moreover, just those of whom this is true that make the impression we notice on the Pagans who come across them, whether in books or in the actual flesh. The impression which they make of "having something" the Pagan has not got, will prove, I

[1] *Floretti*, viii. [2] *Mount Carmel*, Bk. II, vii, 4. [3] II Corinthians, xii, 10.
[4] R.H.J. Steuart, S.J., *The Inward Vision*, p. 119.

think, to be in direct relation to the degree they have reached in this reversal of values.

VII

We may summarize this side of the position in this way: The Pagan feels himself dissatisfied with his own spiritual state and *Weltanschauung*, largely because it does not make him happy, and he believes that personal happiness is the criterion by which life should be judged. He finds to his surprise that certain persons, whose way of life and ideas seem to him mistaken, appear, in spite of this, to be happier and more content than he is. He suspects that they have found, somehow, some secret way of happiness, and he would like to share their secret, but he is not prepared to pay too high a price; he is not prepared to commit himself too much; above all, he must not surrender his own will; it is to be, as to him all life has been, a matter of compromise, of give and take. If he asks to be allowed to share the secret, he is prepared to offer in return a share of goods that he himself possesses, freedom of thought and action, an open mind, an independent judgment; and, to him, his contribution is the greater; but here is a new source of misunderstanding, he finds that the Christian wants nothing from him; he envies him nothing, and will take nothing from him; towards the Pagan he is self-sufficient, and this self-sufficiency is misunderstood.

The Pagan's attitude, as we have defined it, is essentially independent, self-reliant; his approach is as a free man to free men; all relationship must be on an equal footing, and in his relation to the believing Christian he finds that this quality is denied him. He is treated kindly, with consideration, there is every attempt to welcome and understand him, but the footing is not equal in the least. His terms are brushed aside, what he offers is not wanted, what he supposed of great value is ignored; he is given freely, but he cannot buy, and this wounds his self-respect and irritates him; he feels himself and his world depreciated.

He has always paid his way, been self-supporting, he will not be beholden to anybody, he will not accept charity; in nine cases out of ten he rejects it and retreats; if he cannot dictate the terms, he will not parley.

There may be some individual characters who are so deeply Pagan in their hearts, so essentially rebellious and self-assertive, so abnormally sensitive to the slightest yoke, that greater knowledge would but further alienate them. Possibly there have always been such people, perhaps there always will be, who can tell? but they are in a small minority; they are as a rule misfits in whatever circles they move, inharmonious, non-conformist, and discordant; these rebels would be only more rebellious, more deeply and more violently hostile, the more they understood of real religion, the nearer they came to grips with what it meant. They misunderstand less, but combat more, than the great mass of more indeterminate people.

Some way there surely is to meet these rebels, to turn their force from Anti-Christ to Christ, but here we cannot be concerned with them, we are only attempting to explain, to those who are not intentionally hostile, where the differences lie that separate us, and to how large an extent they are quite other than what they are usually supposed to be.

Let us then take again the supposed apparent self-sufficiency of the religious man, his refusal to accept what you offer him, and see what the reason is for his refusal and how it could not well be otherwise.

Two typical examples come to mind, in the fields of science and of higher criticism.

In the first, we all know that there has been a movement in
recent years for leading men of science to abandon the extreme
materialism of their last century's predecessors. Sir James
Jeans speaks of a Great Mathematician behind the mathematical phenomena of Creation. Dr. Eddington holds out
the possibility of an even more humane approach to God,
and there are constant examples of this tendency in new devia-
tions from the laws of Nature; do not even quantums appear
to exert free will, in a way which would have shocked an
older generation of physical science? That this should be so,
is to the religious man quite satisfactory as a tendency, but he
is not as a rule much excited by it. To him the essential fact
of the universe is already established in the fact of God; he
knows that no discovery of science can, if it be sound, contradict that fact, he needs no scientific reinforcement of his
conviction. He knows, for how can he help knowing, that
scientific theories are always changing, that to build on the
theistic findings of Sir James Jeans to-day the structure of one's
belief would be unwise, for the scientist of to-morrow may
reject him. In so far as the findings of to-day agree with the
religious faith from which he starts, he thinks them true, and
likely to prevail ultimately, but they will be subject to the same
ups and downs of controversy, of refutation and question and
alteration, as every other form of human knowledge. His
belief in God is founded, and must be founded, on a far surer
and more enduring basis than that of the twentieth-century
telescope.

This attitude is particularly annoying to the friendly pro-
Christian who hurries up with the news: "See here," he is
saying, "What concessions I have brought you! Even our
best science admits there may be a God! You see how the
difference between us is getting smaller, we have the authority

now of the British Association for approaching you. We can parley with you now without disgrace." And it is as though he announced no news at all, as though he had told them that Queen Anne was dead. He is damped and rebuffed by his reception.

"Yes, quite, very nice, very gratifying, he has got so far as that, has he? Well, we congratulate him, and you too, it is nice for you," they seem to say, "But it does not affect us in the very least. He has found nothing out that we did not know already, nothing, that is, that affects our position."

This chilling and superior attitude, as it appears to the would-be co-operator, may be softened by politeness; more than this, there may be more pleasure expressed, more interest taken, but this is in essentials the response he evokes; there is, as we have admitted, no "give and take."

If we look at the question with the Pagan's eyes we can surely understand the effect upon him. His position may be summarized as follows:

"For years, the conflict between religion and science has been one of the chief obstacles to religious belief for enlightened modern minds. As enlightened modern men, we are bound to follow science where the divergence is definite and extreme. These concessions on the part of scientists make part, at least, of your theory possible, and you do not seem to appreciate at all of what immense importance this is to you. Don't you see that what you have maintained so obstinately against all rational probability for so long, has now, at last, some chance of being true?"

It seems to him that the religious man in his attitude of indifference is showing up his own obscurantism, his under-valuation of intellect and progress, to a degree that finally condemns him. We are back at our old difference of starting point, and the consequent reversal of values it involves.

The Totalitarian Christian is convinced that he knows of God's existence through revelation; he arrives at this conviction in many ways, rational, intellectual, personal, as the case may be. He has already, in all probability, considered the challenge of science among other possible challenges to his beliefs; he has reasoned to the best of his ability, from a variety of kinds of knowledge, external and interior, but, inasmuch as he *is* a Totalitarian Christian, by whatever means he has got to that position, whether by birth and tradition, or by intuitive or intellectual conversion, or by whatever combination of these methods, *as* a Totalitarian Christian, he starts always, in everything, from belief in God, as the supreme knowledge, as the one sure thing; his universe, his life is Theocentric. To him, with his Theocentric basis, it seems fantastic to suppose that this main fact of all existence can be in the slightest degree affected by the opinions of a human being, however eminent, however learned. If the President of the British Association agrees with God, so much the better for him, if he disagrees, so much the worse.

From the Pagan Anthropocentric point of view, we can see that the whole order is reversed, as inevitably it is bound to be. The authority of contemporary science is accepted as absolute, God is the doubtful, fluctuating factor, as with Mr. Curtis and his Commonwealth.

Can these two views ever be reconciled?

Exactly the same situation arises over textual criticism of the Bible, and the recent tendency of the higher critics, supported by the archæologists, to revert to a more orthodox attitude; it arises constantly in moral problems.

We are reminded of President Lincoln's answer, when he was asked if he thought that God was on his side:

"I don't know about that, but I very much hope that I am on God's side!"

Lincoln was not a Totalitarian Christian, but in this answer he is certainly taking the Theocentric position.

VIII

The underlying cause of this recurrent impasse is the lack of understanding, in the non-believer, of the nature of totalitarian belief. To the friendly Pagan we have been considering, the idea of God has ceased to be obnoxious; the Old Man in the sky has ceased to play a part, but His place is taken by so vague a concept that Faith, in the sense in which the Christian means it, is indeed unthinkable. An indeterminate "force for good," an "emanation of our higher selves," the "great mathematical mind," the "movement of integration," "meta-biology," to use but a few of the synonyms which are supposed to clarify and improve our idea of God, cannot inspire us with a real devotion. It is possible to imagine acceptance of these concepts in so far as the words make any sense at all, but it is utterly impossible for such acceptance to play an active part in human life.

When we try to speak of the Love of God as a motive power, meaning of life or main reality, we are talking an unintelligible nonsense, and are met with a corresponding incredulity.

Sometimes it is regarded as a fiction, an artificial and conventional phrase, which we ourselves do not take seriously, sometimes, and more often in these days, there is an attempt to translate it charitably into love of Humanity, or, as they would say for our benefit, "love of our neighbour."

The substitution of the second commandment for the first is one of the chief marks of the New Morality, as is natural, for you cannot love a God who is not there, and to tell you to do so is to court disaster. But it is dangerous to take odd stones out of an arch; has not all heresy consisted in taking parts of truth out of their context, so that, taken wrongly, out of order, what is true in itself becomes untrue? for "All evil is a mistaking of means for ends."[1]

The Christian Divine Order is a whole; the parts all have their places; you cannot pick and choose and interfere without ruining the building. If the Commandments hold, the first is first; if you reject the first, why confront us with the second? They stand or fall together, they are integral to each other.

Love of God and of our neighbour cannot be separated, the attempt to do so, in one form or another, is the most persistent heresy of the day.

It is one of the commonest accusations of the Pagan that religious people, as such, are no better than unbelievers—as, if their claims were true, they ought to be; this lack of conspicuous goodness is a real cause of scandal and we must meet it. The answer to it lies along two lines; in the first place it is not altogether true. Not all religious people behave better

---

[1] Cf., St. Augustine, *epistolae* clv. III.

"If all your prudence, by which you try to watch over human affairs; if all the resolution with which you meet, without fear, the iniquities of which you are a victim; if all the temperance by which you keep yourself uncorrupted in the welter of human corruption surrounding you; if all the justice by the right application of which, you render to each one his due; if all this effort and striving have, as their sole aim, that those to whom you wish well, may be sound in body, and safe and untroubled by the wickedness of anybody—yours will not be true virtues, nor will the happiness of these for whom you exercise them, be true happiness."

than all unbelievers, certainly, but it could be maintained that, class for class, one kind of man as against a similar kind, the one with religion will tend to be more moral than the equivalent type without it; the case is clearer and less disputable if we take examples from the best types only; no Pagan Ideal Man equals the Saint.

That the difference is not outstanding and universal, we must admit and admit it to our sorrow, but the explanation is not difficult to the Christian, it lies in the fallen nature of our kind; we are not now what we were meant to be, we only very imperfectly attain it. We are met with an expectation in the Pagan that Faith should, as by magic, quite transform us, instantly, into our own ideal of sanctity; it does not do so, nor do we expect it, though we realize that it is expected of us. We claim that the means of grace at our disposal should help us to an immense degree towards our object, and that that object itself is higher and much harder to attain than the corresponding aim of our Pagan friends. We would give, as examples of the truth of this, those among us who have reached, or most nearly reached, our common aim; for the rest, we would acknowledge our shortcomings, we would admit ourselves to be most imperfect examples of the ideal type we ought to be.

But, having made all allowance for our imperfection, and the large discrepancy between what we profess and what we do, we are still left with a deep divergence in what we count as "good," in what we would *wish* to be.

When we remark that it is not necessarily his "goodness" which attracts the Pagan's notice to the religious man, what we really mean to say is that he does not find conspicuous the marks of goodness that he recognizes. Our contention here would be that the "bad" Christian does not in fact attract him in the least, he is easily accounted for and neglected; he fits the picture and can be disposed of. The case that we are considering is different, it assumes a type of Totalitarian Christian who has arrested the Good Pagan's attention, who cannot be ignored and swept aside. We have seen that the Pagan envies him as "happy," as having what seem to him peace and security; we would suggest that what he has been struck by is in fact some degree of personal holiness, that this, and this only, has caught his attention although he has no name for such a thing.

It is often asserted that moral principle can be separated from religious faith, and that the large element of agreement which can be found in any age and under every system on certain basic lines of moral judgment is proof of this.

That this is true up to a certain point, nobody would deny. There are certain broad lines of conduct which all human societies approve, others that they condemn. Courage, sincerity, devotion to something beyond oneself are, we may say, universally approved, cowardice, meanness and selfishness, condemned; but when we come to analyse more clearly the comparative assessment of even such basic qualities as these, and the forms of their expression, we find almost infinite variations of judgment, dependent upon the different philosophical outlooks of the different societies concerned.

The two main lines of thought we must consider, might seem at first in very large agreement on the main lines of their moral judgment. Both share the same cultural and temporal background, both build on the same experience of life. We have seen already how the modern Pagan tends to use Christian terminology, to condemn as un-Christian what he disapproves of. To assume the "Christian Ethic" as included in his more complete and wider moral outlook, he is less conscious of opposition than of supersedence. He would say that some aspects of the "Christian Ethic" had depended on a much narrower scientific outlook than that we possess to-day, that certain ascetic and restrictive values which had at one time been supposed essential, could now be seen to have been accidental; all such, he has discarded willingly, but he maintains that what there was of valid and enduring moral value, has been retained, expanded and perhaps reinterpreted in what he would call enlightened modern opinion.

This persuasive and conciliatory proposition it is our unpleasant duty to contradict; here is the essence of the United Front, and of our obligation to refute it.

We must for the moment assume agreement on two propositions; that what we call "goodness," in some form or other, matters, that "good" conduct is preferable to "bad" conduct, and that it is possible to outline, however broadly, and with however many exceptions, general principles on which to judge it.

So far we may agree, but when we come to define our test of what is good conduct, we shall find that the standpoints from which we approach the question, differ so widely that we can make no progress; to call them hostile is an exaggeration, but in practice they are most often in opposition. We find, in fact, the same basic divergence which has met us at every angle of approach, between the Theocentric and Anthropocentric worlds.

The Pagan judges the moral value of conduct by its relation to general human welfare, and he does this so usually and so avowedly that he prefers nowadays to substitute the terms "social" and "anti-social" for good and bad. The Christian, on his side, views it, and must view it, in the light of his Theocentric orientation, as a question of human relationship to God. Goodness for him is not measured by social use, but by conformity with, or deviation from, God's Will.

The strong point of the Pagan's position is obvious; it can be assessed by immediate results, or so nearly immediate as makes no difference; you "do good," and you can see what you have done; it is measurable in terms of "output."

The Christian's test of value is elusive; you cannot assess it quantitatively at all, the emphasis is on being rather than doing, on what you are, and can be, in relation to God; your actions illustrate this, the final value—in themselves they are of comparative unimportance.

> "A Christian ought to rejoice, not because of his good works and virtuous life, but because his life and acts are such solely for the Love of God, and for no other reason whatever."[1]

This attitude is, to the Pagan, irritating; he condemns it as unpardonably subjective, the entire negation, in practice, of our profession to accept and follow objective truth.

He starts from the assumption we have considered, of Man himself as Ultimate Arbiter, what we have termed extreme self-determination; God is to him essentially Man's creation, a figment or projection of his mind, formed and determined by his own needs and wishes; to refer our moral judgment to such a figment is, logically, extreme subjectivism; to him, what we call God's Will is our own will, projected.

That there are forms of religious subjectivism is not denied by Totalitarian Christians, but a very slight study of recognized spiritual teaching would convince the inquirer, if he were indeed objective, that the whole emphasis of totalitarian teaching is directed definitely against such error.

[1] St. John of the Cross. *Ascent of Mount Carmel*, Bk. III, xxvi, 5.

"Je vous réponds que rien n'est plus dangereux ni plus sujet à l'illusion que de se constituer juge des inspirations divines, et que c'est le moyen infaillible de s'égarer en prenant pour la volonté de Dieu tout ce qui nous monte dans le coeur et nous passe dans l'esprit.[1]

"Le vrai dévot s'étudie à remplir parfaitement tous les devoirs de son état et toutes les véritables bienséances de la société. . . . Pourvu qu'il ne fasse pas sa volonté, il est toujours assuré de faire celle de Dieu."[2]

In these two representative passages we can see how clearly such a mistake is guarded against.[3]

The Christian would accept "social" and "anti-social" in general as terms of approval or disapproval, but he would not judge his actions by those terms; he would assume that God's Will in the end is, and must be, the good of man, but he would not assume, as would the Pagan, that all misfortunes and tribulations that befell him were necessarily, by their nature, against that Will, nor even, in consequence, against his own ultimate interests. This is one example of the reversal of values which Totalitarian Christianity demands.

The whole difference between these two conflicting standards is summed up in the alternative ideals of Personal Sanctity or Social Usefulness, with the Saint or the Social Reformer as their types. The conflict underlying this contrast of types is deep and far reaching in its implications; we will try to pursue it further, later on; for our purpose at this point we accept it, as one more illustration of the division

[1] *Manuel des âmes intérieures. Obéissance.* Père Grou, S.J.
[2] op. cit. *La vraie dévotion.*
[3] That what is presented to us as God's Will may be in truth falsely so represented, that is a different question and more difficult to dispute, but we do, even so, receive it objectively. For ultimate justification we are left here, as so often, to the empirical test, does our way or the other way work out best?

between the Christian and the non-believer, and an important source of misunderstanding.

When we begin to consider, in more detail, the differing shades of Pagan thought to-day, we begin to lose ourselves and lose our way; there are so many forms of non-belief, so many stages of rejected value, from militant atheism to the faint pro-Christian, through varying shades of Agnostic Nihilism. In the face of such diversity it seems vain to attempt general conclusions, yet if, collecting up the different strands, we face this incoherent mass of uncertainties with our opposing Totalitarian Christianity, we do see, unmistakably, the main lines of their common agreement as against us.

In all, we have the displacement of God by Man as the central fact of life, as the starting point and goal of our existence.

No difference of politics, of temperament, of environment, can compare in intensity and in depth to this division of allegiance to Man, as ultimate, absolute—or God.

All the misunderstanding from both sides comes in the end from the vastness of this difference, which no attempt to minimize can efface, so difficult, so almost impossible is it to project oneself, in imagination, across the gulf.

For those who have never known a world without God in it, it is hard enough to conceive such emptiness, but from the other side it is still harder.

Has anyone ever met an unbeliever who had any approximate idea of God?

An intellectual concept he may have, something akin to a mathematical point, or a kind of vague and sentimental feeling that is far removed from the Christian's meaning, but the whole notion of the Love of God is without reality or meaning to him.

How can you love a point in mathematics, or a vague something that you think you feel?

"He that cometh to God, must believe that He is."[1]

With this in mind, we should on our side remember that much of our life and our action and our inaction is bound to appear senseless and useless, and even wrong, without the key, which we seem to be so powerless to give. We can only ask for a suspense of judgment; we can only say to the Pagan, in self defence:

"You must understand, on your side, that there is a method in our madness. You may think our way of life and our range of values mistaken, even disastrous, but you must see that the whole hangs together; if we are mistaken, it is one mistake, so immense that our whole being is engulfed, everything stands or falls for us on our one theory, on our one fact, which we call God. What we mean by God is something positive, all absorbing, not to be temporized with or argued with, or allowed so far and no farther in our lives, something whose demands reach out in all directions. We cannot deny a part, we cannot alter or mitigate or dilute the truth we see. We cannot dictate to God how He should act. We cannot think something better than how God wills it, for our idea of 'good' is what He wills."

[1] Hebrews xi, 6.

III

BARBARIZATION

"Thy ways and thy devices have brought these things upon thee."

JEREMIAH iv. 18.

We have in the former pages been attempting to deal with the personal difficulties between the two main lines of mental outlook, which we have called, respectively, "Totalitarian Christian" and "Good Pagan." We have, while emphasizing the fundamental opposition of their basis, yet tried, if we could, to present the conflict clearly, free from the commoner misunderstandings which mutual distrust and ignorance involve. We have brought ourselves in the end to what seems an impasse, almost an abandonment of the attempt at understanding, an agreement on this one point of our complete inability to agree. We believe that that is in fact the only outcome of any clear realization of our difference as regards our personal attitude to life. The medium in which we express our thoughts is different, the criterion by which we measure our own and each other's action, and so, and far more important, is the end that we have in view. But having reached so discouraging a conclusion along these lines, we should, and I think we can, try other mediums in which to communicate with each other, what we might call a more indirect approach.

The most cogent argument to-day, in any question, is the pragmatic or experiential; it brings the abstract, immaterial (what Lenin excludes as "Bourgeois idealism"), into the quantitative, measurable dimension in which most modern minds are more at home. If we can state our case, so far as possible, in terms of purely material advantage, we shall further it far more effectively, with our public, than we could hope to do by the most eloquent exposition of our Faith.

In the latter case we are speaking a language that is foreign and unintelligible to our hearers—to ourselves, it may be "with tongues," but to them, gibberish; we cannot hope to persuade them by such means.

In the method we are now proposing to ourselves, the position will be reversed; we shall try to present our values in their terms; we shall try to support our Totalitarian Revelation of Faith by a purely material practical demonstration of the social usefulness value it contains. In so far as we are ourselves Totalitarian Christians, the language in which we speak is to us foreign, it is not natural to us nor adapted to express the ideas that are to be expressed; we are translating into our hearers' language. We are moreover at a disadvantage from the fact we have already touched upon, of the difference in our ideas of even "social" value. We cannot, in the nature of things, maintain that a Theocentric view of life promotes everything that our opponents consider "good." The current controversies on such immediate questions as divorce and contraception and euthanasia are obvious demonstrations of this fact; here it is useless to minimize our cleavage in the social, as well as in the personal, field; we can only repeat that on these points we differ in fact as to their ultimate usefulness. Our outlook takes a longer time-horizon, and if we accept the test of "social use" as applicable to the questions to be discussed, we must demand, on our side, this extension in the time-consideration that is allowed. We are meeting our opponent on his own ground, with weapons of his choosing, not our own, and we must make one condition for such battle; if we try to meet him on his material values, taking human welfare as our test of "good," temporal human welfare in this world, he must concede to us a time-dimension that is longer, and far longer, than his own. I believe that if he grants

us this, we can make our case that even temporal welfare does
depend, ultimately, upon belief in God, and on the Divine
order that follows from it. We shall admit that on a shorter
view it is not so, that the first immediate result of our rebellion
is, or appears to be, immediate good. We point for illustration
of this truth to the experiment of our First Parents. The
knowledge of Good and Evil they obtained must have
appeared at first as surely good, they were "like gods," or
so it seemed to them, but on a longer view it was not so; we
see it, looking back quite differently, as:

> ". . . Man's first disobedience, and the fruit
> Of that forbidden tree, whose mortal taste
> Brought death unto the world, and all our woe." [1]

II

In making this attempt to express our case in pragmatic
terms, we must try to establish the largest possible measure of
common ground on which to build.

In attempting to find such agreement of principle in the
personal field, we found respect for truth to be our point in
common; in dealing with the public or social field, we can
best find our principle of agreement in a consideration of the
contemporary situation, the "here and now" in which we all
find ourselves.

Here, as elsewhere, we shall meet with differences; to some
points of view certain aspects of the modern world will be
most apparent and significant, while others will find more
significance elsewhere, but we shall, I believe, find a far larger
measure of common opinion in this field than we could find
in the more personal medium.

[1] *Paradise Lost*, I, 1–3.

There is, for example, almost universal agreement that the present state of the world is unsatisfactory, from whichever side of the picture we approach it, in relation to God or to Humanity. There would not have been such agreement before the War. During the nineteenth century the prevailing belief was in continuous Progress; by all the current standards of assessment the world was becoming a better place to live in for an increasing proportion of people living in it. The prevailing scientific ideas of evolution and natural selection, as interpreted in their most mechanical and material sense, all lent support to this idea of inevitable, automatic progress. There was general acceptance of the theory that what was unprogressive, or anti-social, in tendency would be eliminated by the "naturally selective" process of society. What was arrived at thus became in fact an odd travesty of the much despised assertion: "Whatever is, is right," or that "All things work together for good, to them that love God," only, in place of God's Will as ultimate rectifier, and human will as vital in the process, we had the supremacy of mechanism, a blind non-moral, non-living Progressive Force; the human animal was already will-less, a cog, a unit in the vast machine.[1]

The usual interpretation of this conception still embraced

[1] We see one reaction from the impasse that results, in the impulse to identify non-moral force with God, as in the following passage from Bertrand Russell's *Free Man's Worship*.

"But the world of fact, after all, is not good; and in submitting our judgment to it there is an element of slavishness from which our thoughts must be purged. For in all things it is well to exalt the dignity of Man, by freeing him as far as possible from the tyranny of non-human Power. When we have realized that Power is largely bad, that Man, with his knowledge of good and evil, is but a helpless atom in a world which has no such knowledge, the choice is again presented to us: Shall we worship Force, or shall we worship Goodness? Shall our God exist and be evil, or shall he be recognized as the creation of our own conscience?"

much humane and non-material value. The "Good" was still a subject of discussion, "goodness" was still, although illogically, felt as an essential element in progress; selective progress implied moral approval.

The minority who doubted this world-outlook were discounted as obscurantist reactionaries, they were not persecuted; it was assumed that by process of natural and progressive selection such anti-social units would disappear.

How much longer this point of view could have prevailed unchallenged it is impossible now to estimate; the war of 1914–18 checked it violently and decisively.

We can see through the war years this progressive dogmatism still professing, in face of shattering opposition, that the world would be all the better for its upheaval, that natural selection would be manifested in the emergence of a new and far better world-order out of chaos. We see this optimistic spirit consolidated in the formation of the League of Nations, and all the hope and faith dependent on it.

Now denial of possible progress never was a part of the dissentient point of view; according to that also, good can and does come from evil, growth and development can be the outcome of disaster, but, according to the "obscurantist" view, such results as these are far from automatic, they are contingent on a change of will, without repentance there is no amendment, our sin must be acknowledged and expiated; we cannot assume an inevitable "coming right."

From this point of view, we see the League of Nations, however high its purpose and ideals, to have been founded on a false foundation, a scab upon a wound that was not healed; no admission of sin preceded its foundation, no radical change of heart in those who made it, the victorious powers in a victorious war.

The war and its results were in themselves a challenge to the view of assured progress we are describing, but the formation of the League of Nations did provide a pretext for evading it. If it was possible to maintain that a new order had in fact been established as a consequence of the war, the progressive dogma would be vindicated. The years which followed have proved a progressive disillusionment. The Great War is seen, now, not to have ended war; it has not produced a world "fit for heroes to live in." If it has, in one sense, "established democracy," it is not at all in the sense that was intended; a world welcoming Hitler and Mussolini and Stalin belies the expectations of the Progressive.

Something has gone wrong; very slowly, with great reluctance, that conviction has been accepted. Even in areas, such as the Succession States, and social classes which have benefited directly by the war, the fruits of victory are growing bitter.

"Behold in peace is my bitterness most bitter."[1]

It is no new situation that we are faced with.

It is not only in foreign affairs that this sense of things gone wrong is recognized; the increasing dread of war that hangs over us throws emphasis on that feature of the picture, but in our domestic questions, in personal relations, it is increasingly and more openly recognized that all is not as it should be, that somehow, at some point, unaccountably, "things" have taken a wrong direction.

By the more determinedly convinced Progressive this admission will be made most grudgingly, it will only amount, in some cases, to recognition of excessive speed; what has happened, these will say, is indeed progress, only perhaps it has gone with too great a rush, society was imperfectly prepared for the necessary readjustment. This is the attitude particularly in questions of sexual morals and also in the laxity

[1] Is. xxxviii, 17.

of control over the young, where the issue of personal freedom is involved. According to this view, the maximum of personal independence in all directions is to be desired, and in so far as the present situation demonstrates an assertion of such freedom, we must be prepared to recognize its rightness; the incidental inconveniences should be tolerated as inherent in a transitional phase of growth, as atrocities in times of revolution. This is significant of the change which has taken place in public opinion. The Militant Progressive still exists, but he is on the defensive; he no longer counts on general unconditional support.

If we turn from these extreme protagonists of the deterministic point of view, and consider more usual, moderate opinion, we shall find two main lines of dissatisfaction, a sense of insecurity and a sense of loss.

The first may take the form of fear of war, or of some unformulated disaster, threatening to overwhelm and engulf everybody; it implies in some form or other an unpredictable and non-continuous future and the resultant short-term mental outlook.

This state of insecurity, in pre-war days, was confined to the submerged proletariat, or to Barbarian outposts of civilization. There have always been certain sections of society whose hold on existence was precarious, casual labourers, unemployables, tribes on the North-West Frontier of India, Balkan brigands—these were the forms in which, to most ordinary Europeans, this type of existence was exemplified. That such a state of mind should have become general among civilized people of all social classes would have seemed to our grandparents totally outrageous. It is one example of a general movement back to barbarism which we shall consider later as the "proletarianization" of human life.

This general sense of insecurity affects society in various

ways, always in some form of shortening horizon. You cannot look far ahead, you cannot plan, for yourselves or your children or posterity. The kind of small everyday asceticisms to which our fathers were accustomed, which were assumed as part of duty, become unreasonable and unnecessary. Why deprive yourself of an immediate pleasure in view of a future that may never come? Why live within your income or put by for your old age or for your children, when all alike may perish in an air raid?

Increasingly, the emphasis is on here and now; the "here" is smaller and the "now" more fleeting. "Live and make merry, for to-morrow we die," is a possible slogan when the present at least is pleasant, but to-day we find that, in addition to this sense of future insecurity, we have to add immediate dissatisfaction.

The present is not as it should be, not what we are accustomed to, or what we expected, according to our relative positions.

In almost all respects the material position of the working classes has enormously improved in recent years; this holds good in general in spite of unemployment, and in spite of non-proletarian dictatorships. It can be demonstrated by statistics of goods consumed and actual buying power, as well as by general common-sense observation, yet there is probably more active discontent than there has ever been; expectation has so far outstripped attainment, the world is not, after all, what it ought to be, and they have been taught to expect it "fit for heroes." To a very large proportion of these workers the solution of their difficulties will seem still in material progress, only more, and much more, of what they have. They will have inherited later, as always happens, the discarded ideologies of the Bourgeois, but among them also we can discern signs of an opposing orientation, a sense of loss, and regret at something passing, a sense of impoverishment and deprivation.

In all other classes of society this sense of loss increasingly prevails as we go upward in the social scale. To some extent this is the natural outcome of the general reversal of position which has taken place throughout the last twenty years; the spread of a democratic equalitarian revaluation throughout all European civilization is an undoubted fact, it is the natural concomitant of the improvement in what were formerly the more oppressed.

Those formerly in privileged positions are conscious of loss in enjoying less privilege; they can no longer assume as their natural right the advantage which they formerly could assume; they find themselves now forced into competition with outsiders for posts which would once have been reserved for them; the qualities which were their *raison d'être*, on which their claim to privilege was founded, are in fact no longer valued as they were. This is the usual explanation offered for the dissatisfaction of the governing class, and it is true that these factors operate to produce, here too, a sense of discontentment, but I am convinced that this personal sense of grievance is only a small part of the dissatisfaction with which we have to deal.

There have always at all times been discontented people, there have always been people who felt they did not enjoy the advantages to which they were entitled; this state of mind is found, and has been found, in all social classes, but in the heyday of Natural Progress this sense of grievance was accentuated by the contrast it presented with the supposed natural order: "According to the laws of natural selection, I who have so many obvious merits ought to have risen further than I have." The sense of injustice was intensified by the prevailing metaphysical conception.

To-day, this is not the most usual feeling, there is far more than personal disgruntlement in the bewildered sense of things gone wrong. To regret the past, to attach importance to something which is in danger of ending, have always been symptoms of conservatism; it is one of the odd paradoxes of the modern world that, alongside so much expression of advanced opinion, the popular vogue of Left Wing activity, this conservative sense of loss is so far-reaching. People of widely different mental outlooks agree wholeheartedly upon this point; political, even religious, opposition is momentarily in complete abeyance when we are faced with this realization of losing something of great value to our civilization, some essential element of life as we know it, that is going from us, and is now almost gone.

III

We should here try to define with more precision what in fact we mean by the sense of losing something of great value, something we feel essential to our civilization.

We have discarded the purely personal loss of privilege as an inadequate explanation of our meaning, it does us and our fellows less than justice. We do mean something by this sense of loss, something objective and generally recognized, yet if we try to define what we feel ourselves to be losing, we shall find a difference in emphasis in the elements picked out as most important.

Some would say that the moral principles upon which society was based were disintegrating, some would say that the sense of honour, of *noblesse*, in personal conduct was disregarded, some would say that the elements of civilized life were undermined by the appeal to violence and force; others, and more than might have been expected, deplore an increase in pure materialism, and lament the loss of immaterial values. All, in whatever form they may express it, are conscious of some loss of quality, a "fineness," an intangible "being something," which perhaps we had hardly appreciated before. It is always so, and in all connections, that what we are used to we will take for granted, it is only in loss that we recognize our possession. It is well known that, in all ages, each generation has mourned the passing of what is passing and has condemned the superseding culture. The sense of disintegration and decay in the world around us, of deterioration in comparison with past ages, is to be found from the very earliest times; already in the seventh century B.C. Hesiod was lamenting the First Golden race of men, and deploring the depravity of his own time:

> "Oh would that I had not tarried to live thereafter with the fifth race; but had either died before or had been born after; for now in these latter days is the Race of Iron. Never by day shall they rest from travail and sorrow, and never by night from the hand of the spoiler; and cruel are the cares which the Gods shall give them. The father shall not be of one mind with the children, nor the children with the father, nor the guest with the host that receives him, nor friend with friend, nor shall brother cleave to brother as aforetime. Parents shall swiftly age and swiftly be dishonoured, and they shall reproach their children and chide them with cruel words. Wretches that know not the visitation of the Gods! Such as these would not repay their ageing parents for their nurture. The righteous man or the good man or he that keeps his oath shall not find favour, but they shall honour rather the doer of wrong and the proud man insolent. Right shall rest in might of hand and

Ruth shall be no more. The wicked shall do hurt to his better by use of crooked words, with oath to crown them. All the sons of sorrowful Man shall have strife for their helpmate, harsh-voiced strife of hateful countenance, rejoicing in evil."[1]

And ten centuries later St. Cyprian bewails a very similar state of things as characteristic of his epoch:

> "The world now bears witness to its approaching end by the evidence of its failing powers . . . the peasant is failing and disappearing from the fields, the sailor at sea, the soldier in the camp, uprightness in the Forum, justice in the courts, concord in friendship, skill in the arts, discipline in morals."[2]

When we consider such indictments of past ages, in terms so like what we ourselves should use to-day, we begin to wonder whether the great past, which we are now regretting, was actually very different from the present; are we not perhaps idealizing what is lost, as sentimentalists will idealize the dead?

There is a certain danger, no doubt, of this, and also of distrusting what is new just because it is new and unknown and strange to us; those of us who are now in middle life may, like the Master Builder, be afraid when we hear the new generation knock on the door, but our observations are not limited to age-groups.

One of the most marked features of post-War mentality is the wish to standardize and label, to divide into groups by age or social status, or any other arbitrary measure, as though we were grading goods or market produce. We are used to the terms "age-group," "wage-group," and so on; there is a large choice of grades and sub-divisions, but men and women, as such, have no existence, they must conform to some collective form. This is a vicious and misleading method, and in the

---

[1] Hesiod. *Works and Days*, 174-201.
[2] St. Cyprian. *Ad Demetrianum, III.*

present case it will not help us. It is true that those of us who can remember with any vividness the pre-War years are naturally more conscious of what has changed than younger people whose only means of comparison with the present is second-hand, through what their elders tell them, but it would not be true to deduce from that a proportional curve of regret-prevalence and age. The convinced progressive is oftener old than young; there are many young obscurantists and traditionalists.

It would be more possible, if we should wish to do so, to trace out a temperamental correspondence; those in whatever age- or wage-group who are herd-minded, less individual and less fastidious, will regret the old order less, if they regret it at all; certain types of mind will tend to acclimatize and thrive under the changed conditions of existence, others, who may actually have known no alternative, may wilt and shrink from such an alien world. We admit, then, that subjective elements, the resentment of the formerly privileged, the dislike of change in those who are growing old, the temperamental shrinking from the herd, do affect our attitude to the world around us, and do so in very varying degrees, but none of these are adequate explanations of the deep and widespread dissatisfaction with how things are, and still more with how they are going, which we find in every class and age and temperament; and, combined with dissatisfaction, there is alarm.

It is probably true that, to every generation, its own time has appeared momentous, the changes it itself experiences have seemed exceptional and of great importance; yet, allowing for elements of prejudice, it is true that, in the long process of development and decay which we call history, some periods do stand out as changing more violently than others; the rhythm of ebb and flow, change and decay, does not proceed in uninterrupted pattern. As in individual lives there is

constant change, the process of growing up, of fluctuating
maturity, and of old age, being interrupted at times by sudden
crises and catastrophes, marriage and sudden death and moral
conflicts, so, in the life of nations and mankind, the rate of
change and growth is spasmodic and variable.

Taking all considerations into account, it seems likely that
those of us who are living now, are in fact living through one
of these periods of crisis, that the changes and problems and
upheavals of which we feel ourselves to be the victims may
truly be more than the average readjustments which each
generation is called upon to make.

It is one of the principal fallacies of our age to attach too
great importance to external circumstances, to ignore the
interior and less obvious influences; we are not dependent on
our circumstances or environment, we are not mere products of
our nation and century, yet all these external factors do affect us.

Things happen or do not happen in the external world and
the lives and outlooks of individuals are affected by these
events just as truly as the events themselves are affected by
individuals. If this is so, it is to be expected that an external
event of the magnitude and enormity of the war of 1914–18
should have altered the normal pace and rhythm of human
development, and that we may regard ourselves with reason
as living in a period of transition. The usual tendency to-day,
however, is not to ignore but to exaggerate this truth. From
opposing points of view the post-War world is regarded as
starting fresh, divided from its past.

This is obvious in Russia and in Germany, where the idea
of Revolution succeeds War as the line of demarcation between
past and present. Thought of in this way, it is, of course, a new
era of hope and glory which starts fresh on the ashes of a burnt-
out civilization. This outlook exists in France and England

also, amongst the adherents of Left Wing principles, but it is with its opposite that we are concerned as more characteristic and more interesting.

We find, in the ranks of the moderate and regretful, an equal tendency to regard the War as the whole cause of the successive epoch; a new evil has manifested itself, an unlooked-for, unpredictable misfortune has fallen upon a progressive world and has destroyed it. Communism, and, still more clearly, Fascism, are manifestations of this unfamiliar evil.

It is our contention that this is a false conception, based on a misreading of both past and present. We maintain that the rapid change we are contemplating has not been caused, but only accelerated, by the War; that the tendencies which are alarming public opinion, the emergence of violence and barbarism in all the forms in which they now confront us, the decadence and collapse of private moral values, the vulgarization and degradation of life in general, are not, as is so generally asserted new and quite unaccountable post-War symptoms, but that all this we are now experiencing is but an intensified and enormously speeded-up expression of a process which had begun long before.

We would say that the Great War was in this respect like an illness which discovers and takes advantage of weakness already latent in the organism of the victim. If the germ had not fastened on him at that moment, he might have continued longer without knowing that in fact his heart was weak, or his lungs affected, but he could not have avoided the knowledge indefinitely.

> "In tragic life, God wot,
> No villain need be! Passions spin the plot;
> We are betrayed by what is false within." [1]

[1] George Meredith, *Modern Love*, xliii.

We have in our earlier pages attributed the downfall of the Good Pagan to his failure in relation to the outcast; it is this aspect of the situation that we propose to consider here more in detail. In what way has this overthrow been taking place? In what form has the outcast taken his revenge?

Our suggestion is that our present situation is itself, in part, that revenge; it is the domination of society by precisely those disregarded elements, the outcast, the barbarian, the proletarian, who were not assimilated or civilized or appeased by the culture of enlightened Paganism, but who have been inevitably armed and strengthened and aroused by the process of equalitarian self-assertion, combined, as it is, with increasing mechanization. In the industrial age in which we live, the barbarian too has been industrialized; he is no noble savage, wild and free, he is the victim of his circumstances. The proletarian of whom we so often hear is in fact but the barbarian of the town. In the changing character of our civilization, it is his influence that we recognize, and it is our argument that this emergence, this rise to power, of the proletarian element in life is directly due to the Good Pagan's failure.

IV

We have so far considered the Good Pagan only in opposition to the Christian, we must look at him now in relation to the Barbarian.

We have seen that, compared to the Christian, he stands for moderation, for perfection in a limited field of action, for an essentially attainable ideal as opposed to the limitless Totalitarian concept. We have seen that in one sense the Pagan concentration on human perfectibility here and now has resulted, as he would claim it must result, in progress and development in this field, that the highly developed humanistic Pagan can be taken as the perfection of the Natural Man, and the society which he dominated was in many respects an example of human achievement.

We see that what we must call the first phase of rebellion did result, as was predicted for it, in a general increase of human welfare, even, we may admit, in a certain sense, in an increased individual valuation, an intensified emphasis on personal merit, the aristocratic element supreme.

This is the effect which all good rationalists proclaim as natural from their point of view; according to them, however, it should continue to develop and progress in this direction; it is our contention that it could not do so, that this first stage was, in essence, transitory, that it contained in itself its own destruction, that what has followed was in fact bound to follow.

There is a famous passage in Ibsen's *Rosmersholm* which we might quote in illustration of our point. The hero and heroine are about to drown themselves, but, before they do so, they explain their act: "There is no God above us, therefore we must do justice on ourselves!" They then proceed to commit suicide. This scene produced a great impression when the play first appeared, though not in the sense in which we quote it here. We suggest that there was a deeper meaning in it than Ibsen realized.

The characteristics of the proletarian era in which we appear to be engulfed to-day, seem at first sight to be so diametrically opposed in their whole nature to this earlier form of noble paganism that it may seem a paradox on our part to link them together as phases in one process, but it is precisely this we mean to do. We must first define our "Proletarian."

In all societies there is an element of unsuccessful, non-

excelling, undifferentiated populace; the forms in which this
element is expressed will vary greatly according to the framework of each culture. Sometimes its existence is recognized
and dealt with as an alien element as was the case in ancient
civilization, in the divisions between Greek and Barbarian,
Roman Citizen and Alien, Slave or Free. Sometimes, as in
our own Humane Paganism, the existence of such an element
is ignored; but, by ignoring, you do not eliminate it.

We are not suggesting that in practice the ancient slave
population was individually inferior to the dominant ruling
race; we know that the Greek slaves imported into Rome were
to a large extent the means of culture, that Epictetus was in
name a slave; what we mean to suggest is the general principle
which the theory of oligarchic rule implies, of a subject class
of less-developed people to whom the rights of equals do not
apply.

Taken in the widest sense, and not to be identified with any
existing divisions of social class, there are, in the material
world, such people, unassimilable by the civilization to which
they at any rate nominally belong.

The principles of Enlightened Paganism, the freedom and
self-determination and tolerance which we associate rightly
with Liberalism, are only workable without such people;
a "gentleman's agreement" only holds among "gentlemen."

The different names applied at different times to designate
this human residue indicate the varying aspects in which we
regard it; to the Hellene, the Barbarian, to the Jew, the Gentile,
to the Free Citizen, the Bondsman, to the Intellectual, the
Philistine, to the Gentleman, the Proletarian—always, ultimately, the same division between the chosen people and the
outsider, the people who count and fit in, and those who
do not.

In all these cases we must recognize that a different standard rules within the group, different relations between man and man, different expectations and demands upon each other.

We have seen that the old Pagan civilization did recognize the existence of the outcast, did incorporate and include him as a slave, but this was inadequate recognition; it acknowledged the problem but it did not solve it, and through failure to solve the problem adequately that civilization also perished. The parallel between our own time and the end of the Roman Empire has been pointed out very often, recently; the sense which is so prevalent to-day of impending catastrophic changes in the world and the passing of European order as we have known it, attracts our attention to other catastrophes, other changings of world orders in the past, and the fall of the Roman Empire is an example which shows striking similarities with our own situation.

Professor Rostovtzev has shown in his *Social and Economic History of the Roman Empire* that the collapse of the Roman world in the third century coincided with just such a social situation, a depopulation of the countryside, overcrowded cities of derelict unemployed, emergency measures for dealing with these town proletarians, not coercion or suppression as in earlier days, the ruthlessness of the Slave Revolt times is absent, but free bread, free education and free games, the desperate unconstructive propitiation with which we are familiar in our day.

On paper it must have seemed to progressive Romans that the march of social progress was assured, that the poor and dispossessed were receiving justice long overdue, and that all would soon come right, because it must; yet we know from the writings of contemporaries that the upper-class intellectuals were uneasy, that they felt, as we do now, that the crash

was coming, that bread and circuses were all in vain to avert
the magnitude of the disaster. And we see, looking back at
that time down the perspective of 1700 years, that they were
justified in their foreboding, that the structure of their society
was unsound, that they were doomed to go under as they
did. We see the old culture of the Pagan world fighting an
inevitably losing battle against the proletarian barbarization of
life.

It is customary to despise the later Romans, to pronounce
them decadent and corrupt, and leave it there; no doubt in
part they were, and so are we. The more we study them
and their situation, the more we shall recognize our likeness
to them. They, like ourselves, were the end of a great tradition,
they were living, as we are, on a dying past; their outlook was
made up, as ours to-day, of a strange and often illogical
mixture of old and new, a clinging to the past that made us
great, with a half deliberate repudiation of it. A sense that
it was no good to look behind, that the dead must bury their
dead, with a fear and loss of nerve in facing the future; and
we see above all in the fall of Rome the defeat of the ancient
Pagan by the outcast; he too, as we to-day, was overcome,
submerged, and swept aside by the uprush of undealt-with
barbarism, not, as was once so conveniently supposed, an
unlooked-for, unprovoked attack from Goths and Huns, but
the rotting of the fabric from within which we are facing at the
present day.

A minority can impose, and often has imposed, its ideas
and standards on the indifferent mass, but, to do so, it must
be aware of its position; it must know itself and accept its
obligations.

Our newer Paganism failed in this respect to a far greater
extent than did its prototype. The ancient world was more

realist, more clear-sighted; its Paganism was not diluted and neutralized by Christian ethics, as is the modern form. This difference, which would usually be advanced in favour of the modern variant, is, to our mind, a further condemnation of it. We would say that the present form of Paganism, the enlightened, pseudo-Christian compromise, is based essentially upon an unreal foundation, and is therefore fundamentally unsound and doomed to fall.

The ancient Pagan recognized the slave, he admitted sin and evil and their consequences; his recognition and his admission were imperfect, and, through their imperfection, he has failed, but he was feeling forwards, not regressing, his outlook was not founded on rejection.

In the half-conscious background of the Modern, the Christian ideology exists, questioning and disturbing his conclusions, upsetting the balance of his Paganism; he is forced continually to evade the truth, to betray a struggling element of conscience, to proclaim his position as what it is not, to deny the reality he will not face.

We have seen that the ancient Pagan Democracy was based upon an underworld of slaves, and in the earlier stages of our Pagan revival the same was true in a lesser degree; there were not actual slaves to buy and sell, but the great mass of the uncivilized were yet in complete material subjection to the humane *élite*. The democratic principle prevailed only within a limited chosen circle; it was self-determination for the Aristocrat.

The Good Pagan is essentially aristocratic; his whole outlook and behaviour presuppose a position of privilege and dominance, but the disadvantage of his new manifestation showed itself clearly here. The new Pagan started in revolt against the Christian order, in which the essential supernatural value of every human soul had been proclaimed, and it was intrinsic to his whole position that he included all the Christian "good," in improved form, in his new Paganism. If, in the ultimate spiritual order of the Christian, there was known to be neither Greek nor Barbarian, neither bond nor free, he must assert the same of his temporal order.

It followed, therefore, that he must proclaim the temporal equality of mankind, and this in the face of all experience, of all the rational demonstration, on which he professed to base his attitude.

There was a contradiction and conflict, from the outset, in the very principles on which he counted. Under no system, and at no period, have men been equal in physical attributes, as animals, nor yet as rational beings, as equality proclaimed in a world of material values must imply.

The Good Pagan was sincere in his assertion; if his premises were correct as he believed them, if the whole value of the Christian world could be preserved, improved, without God in it, then the principle of equality must hold good translated, like all else, into material value, and, basing his attitude on this supposition, he rejected every contrary indication.

In the same spirit of convinced rejection of every challenge to his fixed assumptions he has shirked or denied the whole problem of evil: the sinner, the failure, the outcast, the world that is unredeemed. He has superimposed upon the rejected picture an ideal picture of his own, an ideal world, of reasonable perfectable human beings co-operating for the common good. In order to substantiate his ideal picture, he must rule out incongruous elements, there is no room in his world for the misfits. His whole system is based on denial of barbarism, but by denying evil you do not eliminate it, by calling sin social maladjustment you have not cured it, by denying the need for salvation you have not saved the world.

Shut in, as we find him, in his unreal world of reasonable, enlightened gentlemen, he is wilfully unconscious of his position. Surrounded on every side by the non-conformist enemies of his culture, pressing upon him, claiming recognition, he persistently puts his glass up to his blind eye; he leaves the door of his citadel wide open in order to prove that there is no danger there.

We see in the overthrow of the Good Pagan an illustration of both his weakness and his strength, his lack of realism and his sincerity. We may say that he is dying for his beliefs.

It is easy to run him down in his defeat, it is easy to be wise after the event. Do not let us underestimate his value. Those of us who have grown up from childhood among the best examples of such Good Pagans could never, I believe, make that mistake. There is in the finest Paganism a nobility which perhaps cannot be equalled anywhere. The complete sinking of self in public duty, the courage in face of an insensate world with no belief in an enduring justice, no "friend behind the phenomena" at all—to us who have known such characters, admiration for the Good Pagan must endure through all conviction of his present failure, but the weakness in his position is inherent; his overthrow was implicit in his beginning.

v

In the foregoing chapter we have attributed the Good Pagan's failure to the fundamental illusion from which he starts, the belief that it is possible to conserve all of positive and constructive value in the Christian order while removing from it the belief in God. We have seen this assumption of the unimportance and irrelevance of God to underly a great deal of modern thought; we have seen it in Mr. Huxley's treatment of the Mystics and in the whole theory of the United Front; we believe it to be the ultimate mistake, the most complete totalitarian falsehood, we believe this primal false idea to be responsible, in some form or other, for almost all our present-day disasters, and that we are able to recognize its effects in numbers of seemingly separate consequences. It is our contention that, if we follow back these various forms of division to their beginning, we shall find that in every case we return to the same source, the repudiation of belief in God. We shall find that, in practice, this one "great refusal" does affect all sides and aspects of our life, our aims, our values, our own personal nature.

Such inquiry may be followed on two lines which we may roughly class as inner and outer. The inner, affecting questions of final value, more intangible, more personal, more illusive, as to the effect from within of belief in God, we have touched upon already earlier and shall refer to again in later chapters. It is the outer or structural aspect of the difference that we must consider here, its effect upon us as social beings.

We have formulated, so far, our opposing types as Totalitarian Christian and Good Pagan, the corresponding social attitudes we may style "hierarchic" and "equalitarian."

To define the Good Pagan as equalitarian may seem at first sight a contradiction to the charge of aristocratic limitation already made against him, but we are doing so deliberately. The equalitarian principle is essential to the enlightened Pagan point of view, although in practice such equality be limited to the selected circle. It is our contention that it was, in fact, adherence to the equalitarian theory which led to the fatal ignoring of the outcast, precisely because with such material the equalitarian theory would not work.

If we ascribe the Good Pagan's overthrow to ignorance of

the proletarian, failure to recognize his existence as a danger and the consequent lack of defence against his onslaught, the form in which this overthrow has occurred we can find in the progress of democracy, taken, as we have taken all our terms, in its exact and literal meaning. To the casual speaker "Democratic" has a vaguely pleasant sound, it suggests fair play and good sense, an absence of swank or side; it is comfortable, homely, English, hardly more, but the true meaning is there all the same, a sinister meaning if we look into it, detached from comfortable associations. The rule of the crowd, of the mob, nothing more, nothing less; not, be it noted, social justice, not fair play for under-dog, but just mob-rule.

It is in this sense that we use the term when we say that the Good Pagan's overthrow has been the result of democracy, the putting into practice more and more of the ideal theories of his world of dreams.

Under the older forms of government, both Christian and the earlier Pagan, it was admitted that an individual from any social level might raise himself through his personal effort, there were no insurmountable barriers to such a rise, but it demanded personal quality. There are countless examples of this rise in class throughout the Middle Ages, and in all ages that process has gone on and been encouraged; the lives of many eminent Victorians illustrate such a rise; the means by which they raised themselves in status were varied and not always admirable, but always personal quality of some sort was the deciding factor.

La carrière ouverte au talent presumes *talent.*

This principle was in accord with an earlier Pagan's oligarchic order, a struggle against adverse circumstances won from him wholehearted admiration. There was no danger to the oligarchy from such an upward move of excellence; it could and did retain its character, and the new members gratefully absorbed it. What happens now is entirely different; the principle of control has shifted gradually from a quality to a quantity standard; the element of personal merit has diminished; numbers *qua* numbers have become decisive.

The recent extensions of the suffrage illustrate this; a suffrage qualified by the mere fact of existence. It is easily arguable that the old property qualification for voting was faulty; a man does not become wise nor a good politician by owning something, but the fact that he owns nothing does not make him wise either; universal unqualified suffrage is fatalistic, it is indeed a counsel of despair. It means that in the political sphere the overwhelming balance of power and decision lies with the crowd, the undifferentiated proletarian masses whose strength is in quantity and quantity only, who are not, in the nature of things, fit to govern; it is the abdication of the governing class, the abandonment of all attempt at quality-value. This principle we shall find in all departments of life, for, in the last resort, all life is one, and far the most serious and far-reaching aspect is the mental and moral change that it implies.

In any society its moral judgments are largely affected by its public opinion; this is doubly so in a Pagan civilization, where human opinion is acknowledged as final and there is no other law to test it by. Under the dominance of the Good Pagan, public opinion was set by his standards, its influence was mainly strong and good and moral; but under the rule of the crowd it is crowd opinion which forms the ideas of the modern world, and the crowd is, in essence, undifferentiated, without quality, without merit or excellence.

Persons of merit individually are, in and as the crowd, obliterated. We find our ideas, our principles, are formed on the basis of a majority judgment; "what most people think" is taken as "what is right."

It is inevitable that a governing class values the qualities through which it governs. The Good Pagan, as we saw, assessed himself by a high standard of value, but it was the value in which he himself excelled; in crowd rule the whole emphasis is on quantity and quantity only, because on such a basis alone can the crowd prevail. According to our view, the displacement of quality by quantity is a natural and inevitable stage in the reversal of the natural order, the disintegration of society which follows from interference with its unity, but we admit that external circumstances do influence, and in this case have influenced, our condition. We have seen that the war of 1914-18 has had a deep and disastrous effect upon us in increasing and speeding up the process of progressive disintegration which was already operating in us; another factor of very great importance has been the increasing mechanization of life, and our increasing dependence on the machine.

The greater part played by mechanical process, the more will value be concentrated on mere output, for the essence of machine mass-production is precisely this substitution of the quantity standard for the old standards of good workmanship. The individual man is depreciated under mass-rule, in favour of the crowd, and the individual product is superseded by mass production of a standardized object.

We have seen that any dominant group holds as essential those qualities which entail its dominance; the crowd-strength is enormously reinforced by general dependence on the machine. The larger the part played by the machine-idea, the surer and deeper will be the crowd's domination.

This is quite natural and inevitable; the machine is essentially equalitarian, it obliterates variation and pre-eminence; "standard" and "below standard" are its only measures, it is the ideal reinforcement of mob-rule.

The degree to which the mind of the present day is dominated by the crowd and crowd values is seen in the influence of the cinema. No film can be produced profitably unless it appeals to about two million people, yet the cinema has more cultural influence than any other form of art. Those of us who belong to the old culture are obliged, if we go to the cinema, to see what the crowd wants to be seen; the same is true, to a lesser degree, of the theatre and the daily press. "What the public wants" is the criterion in every field of cultural production, and the "public" is the crowd, not the *élite*.

The process we have been describing may be defined perhaps most clearly as "proletarianization"; it is a reversal of positions and values, but distinct and essentially different from revolution. Revolution also implies reversed positions and a turning upside down of accepted standards, but it is in itself, in essence, an achievement. It is something thought of and planned and executed by individuals, it is always, if successful, oligarchic, the work of a picked few, of leaders and rulers, using, no doubt, mass-movements and herd-emotions, but using them deliberately, to achieve certain thought-out aims.

Take the two great revolutions of our time, the French and the Russian; what part had the true proletariat in either? One oligarchy replaced another, with violence and bloodshed and mob-emotion. The successful oligarchy in each case used the herd-mind more skilfully and efficiently than its predecessor, they attached more importance to it, studied it more, but the complicated social ideas involved were in no sense herd ideas, they were highly intellectual specialized theories; the minority mind imposed on the majority. So it must always be in revolution.

In proletarianization this is not so; the influence of the herd, of the proletariat, need make no effort, need exert no skill. If the stage is set for it and conditions favour, it rises gradually, spreading and permeating from below upwards through all branches of life, like damp rising and spreading through a great building without a damp course. No one has planned it or done it, no one is responsible; it is without purpose or intention that it happens; automatically, will-lessly, like the rising damp, it spreads and undermines our civilization, and as in the damp building there is no fixed moment at which the structure is ruined, yet gradually it has become uninhabitable, so is our contemporary society being ruined, rotted and undermined from its foundations, by the gradual and certainly increasing influence of the barbarian elements within it.

VI

In the proletarianization of life we may observe several different aspects of one basic process, the gradual and increasing transference of value, from the conscious, individual, intentional element, through varying intermediate phases, to mechanical, helpless, sub-human fatalism; from the long horizon of continued purpose, through ever-diminishing and contracting vistas, to the atomic, hand-to-mouth attitude, familiar to us at the present day.

We see a progressive shortening of vision, a progressive shirking of responsibility, progressive insistence on material value in an ever-narrowing and more limited sense, until in the end we have made a full circle.

The original self-assertion of the Pagan rejected his dependence upôn God as degrading to the dignity of Man; we find him, in the present situation, dependent upon blind mechanical forces. He has rejected superhuman guidance in favour of servitude to the sub-human. God has been replaced by the Machine.

We are all familiar with this attitude, as conspicuous in contemporary ideas.

"I can't help it. I was made like that!" is the typically modern reaction to a challenge; or,

"A person of my sort must think as I do . . . naturally, born in such a place and time, subject as I am to such an environment, I am bound to think and want what I do think and want."

This is the consciously accepted basis of all our present-day social outlooks; we find it openly avowed in Marxist determinism, we find it only less definitely expressed in the general outlook of moderate public opinion; we find it assumed as a foregone conclusion in most excellent measures of social action—housing must be improved, not because it is wrong and unjust that slum conditions should exist, when some are rich, but because people in bad houses become bad; health must be improved for the same reason; people with unsound bodies will be unsound. Now we are not for one moment depreciating the advantage of good housing and good health when we say that this reasoning is fallacious.

It is wrong that people should live under slum conditions because it implies injustice and avarice on the part of the rich, it is the sin of the rich, not the hardship of the poor, that is the most serious element in the situation; if the same conditions and the same hardships occurred from natural causes, the harm involved would have been negligible. As it is, the wrong is there and must be dealt with, but let us know what we are doing and why we do it; good done on a wrong basis may be useless. You do not make people good by good conditions any more than they become bad in adversity. If absence of moral excellence were found only among the very poor or ill we might be persuaded by the Communist that human nature will come right if once the economic basis of life is right, that you cannot expect either virtue or happiness among the exploited victims of capitalism, but we do not find that this is, in fact, the case; the morals of the rich are often bad, so are the morals of the middle class, they too are often unhappy and anti-social; and on the other side we are confronted with the lives of Hermann the Cripple unfit to live from birth, if ever cripple was, and St. Bernadette of Lourdes in our own times, the child of unemployable rag-pickers, doomed both by heredity and environment, it would seem; and countless numbers of unknown noble souls in every condition of adversity.

This externalization of our troubles, this projecting responsibility for our actions increasingly on to outer circumstances, is a conspicuous tendency of our time, the degree to which it is accepted as scientific is typical of the machine-dominated mind, but the impulse to blame outward circumstances for short-comings in ourselves is no new thing, it is but a natural weakness of human nature.

We see here as in so many other cases that an inclination with which we are confronted as typical of our modern post-War world, is not in fact new at all, it is as old as is the human race, what *is* new, or if we prefer it "modern," is the attitude taken up in regard to such inclination. What used to be faced as "sin" or "human weakness" is now accepted by the "modern mind" as harmless or, it may be, admirable.

In this connection we should now consider what is actually implied by this term "modern," which is used so generally as our final sanction; in current use it is replacing Christian as a general term of unquestionable approval; what does it really mean? "The only and most modern hotel in the Cathedral Square," may present us with other difficulties in logic, it is at least easy to see that, in such a context, the term "modern" expresses quite definite advantage. A "modern" hotel is assumed to provide adequate comforts of a material kind, such as running water in bedrooms, central heating and lifts; telephones in bedrooms are clearly "modern." This use of such a word is reasonable, but when we apply the same word to ideas, or human minds, what justification have we for such use?

In one sense, of course, it is tautologous, if by "modern" we mean simply contemporary, the word applies to all living people whatever views they hold on any subject, whatever kind of people they may be; in such a sense it has no value-meaning, but in practice we know it is not used in this sense. In practice it is used to designate one particular type of mind or idea or outlook which is shared by the user, and assumed by him to be of unquestioned merit.

"The modern mind demands," or such and such a theory is "unacceptable to the modern mind," does, if we consider, call before us quite a definite picture of the kind of mind.

It suggests, undoubtedly, concrete quantity-value, a rejection of immaterial, spiritual considerations, a short-distance, quick-return calculation, it also implies the determinist supposition, that we call mechanistic or sub-human, and that they would prefer to call scientific.

We have seen that; applied, rightly, to an hotel, the word implies mechanical advantage; it applies in this sense equally to motor-cars, or engines, or aeroplanes; there is no question that, in all such cases, modern is rightly used in approbation.

Mechanical invention is progressing in its own sphere unquestionably, but are we prepared to maintain that human progress can be assessed by the same formula?

Is not this application of the term "modern," as expressing approval of the human being, but another example of mechanization, the imposing of the sub-human, the automatic, upon the individual and immaterial value?

To a dominant class whatever has brought its own domination is progress. In a proletarian quantity-value society like the present, these elements alone count as progressive. We shall find this tendency to identify quantity or mechanical improvement with progress in every department of our "modern" life.

We shall also find, if we pursue it further, that in this, too, however unwittingly, the Good Pagan has prepared his own overthrow.

VII

We have seen that it was the Good Pagan's contention that his concentration upon here and now, the removal of his treasure from the Heavenly to the Earthly city, had resulted in increased energy and effort, an increased sense of social responsibility; he would say: "You put off the responsibility on to God for what went wrong, as well as for what went right; I take it on myself. If I am prepared to take the blame myself for what goes wrong, I shall quite obviously take more personal trouble to see that it goes right."

This seems a very reasonable contention, and we have admitted that, to a large degree, it was so in the beginning; we have seen that there did seem to be, at first, an access of vitality and zeal, and that it is difficult to point to a precise moment when this activity subsided or began to change from the individual personal effort phase into the present automatic determinism.

How do we come full circle, as we assert, through over assertion of our own free will, to far more complete abandonment of our will than the religious framework had demanded?

We must here define two complementary movements by which this reversal or revolution has taken place.

There has been on the one hand the external overthrow of the Humane Pagan, the swamping of his influence by numbers, the "liquidation" of the aristocrat by the mob; that is the most obvious and straightforward explanation, corresponding to the Barbarian sack of Rome, but it is not, in our view, the most important. We maintain that this external process has been accompanied and accelerated by a corresponding interior disintegration in the quality of the Good Pagan in himself, a parallel to the internal decadence of Rome. He has, without knowing it, become himself infected with the mentality and standards of the crowd.

Nowhere is this change more noticeable than in the current assessment of moral "good," the transference of our ideal from Saint to Social Reformer, from Personal Sanctity to Social Use.

To the modern, personal holiness has no meaning; it is not particularly repugnant to him, but the expression has, for him, no bearing on any aspect of life that he recognizes. If we place before him our two ideal types, Saint and Reformer, he will identify them; "real saints are all reformers," he will say: if they are not reformers, then for him they are not saints.

The extreme example of this attitude is seen in the presentation of Christ as social reformer, with which we are, most of us, familiar. The paradox into which such reasoning leads us logically is illustrated in the following passage from *Studies in Christianity* by the late Mr. Clutton Brock:

"We cannot understand it (the crucifixion), unless we see it as a failure ... unforeseen, disastrous, undesigned. It would have been better if Christ could have lived and taught, and converted the Scribes and Pharisees. It was a waste that he should die so young, as the early deaths of Mozart, and Schubert and Keates are a waste. The world lost all that he might have said and done; think otherwise, and surrender your reason."

For the modern mind, even holiness must be quantitative, it must be assessable in material output of good done. There is, for it, no "being," only "doing," and doing must be concrete and measurable. This is a field in which we can see clearly the change and disintegration in the Good Pagan's attitude, the way in which his own standard and moral value has been influenced from below.

We have seen that he stood in all things for moderation, and this moderation-value was emphatic in his choice and definition of the "Good Man"; here too, he attempted to combine two conflicting standards. Personal integrity and virtue had for him a positive and quite immaterial value, almost, it would seem, as an end in themselves. It would matter how you behaved on a desert island though no one would ever know or profit by it, that he would still maintain, illogically; being as against doing was still important; to be a good man was part of doing good. In these respects his standards approximated, externally, very nearly to the Christian's, as it was his assertion that they would, but if we analyse his ideal "Good Man," we shall find that the basic change has taken place; he performs his good action, he lives his good life, for the ultimate glory of Man, and not of God.

The first decisive step has been taken in the direction of materialization, the Creator has been replaced by the creature.

When you assess your Good Man by social usefulness, you

are, in the same act, discounting his other value as secondary; you are reducing him and yourself to a quantity standard, you are emphasizing, in your very praise of your hero, the opposing and destructive principle to which his existence is, in itself, a challenge.

In output, no individual can compete with the machine; the greater importance we attach to output, the more will machine-mentality affect us.

We see, in fact, how, at the present day, the cult of the Good Man has relapsed into the Dictator who stands or falls by the crowd's approbation, managed and treated as a vast machine.

When you have reduced your Good Man to his output level, you have deprived him of the element in which his virtue lay, he has become an inferior machine. We see this immediate inferiority of the human in a thousand obvious examples so soon as the output test is applied to them.

What is the Marathon runner's speed output, beside the most inferior motor-car? How is the fastest and most skilful craftsman at once outdistanced by the factory?

A machine civilization is essentially proletarian in character because the machine neutralizes natural excellence and puts the unskilled on a level with the skilled.

Even in the handling of the machine itself, the element of skill and personal merit is deplored. We have an example of this in the increasing proportion of cars that are fitted each year with self-changing gear devices. The skilful driver who changes gear well, enjoys practising his skill in changing gear, the incompetent driver prefers to have it done for him, so that he ceases to be at a disadvantage in comparison with his more efficient rival. The number of poor drivers is of course greater than that of good ones, and so the bad driver's wishes must prevail; more and more cars each year are made self-changing, and the good driver loses his distinction in the interest of his inferior, or lazier, fellow.

This element of laziness is important. We have seen that the machine eliminates more and more the need for skill; it also eliminates the need for effort, and this is perhaps the most far-reaching and most disastrous of its results; it is here that we can find the explanation of the seemingly contradictory consequences of the Pagan civilization and its sequel.

We have seen that the mechanistic, automatic attitude seems at first sight the complete contradiction of the Good Pagan's characteristics. In considering the significant change from Saint to Reformer, and following it through the intermediate stages of Humanist Good Man, we have studied the change of ideal of our Good Pagan from one aspect; let us now consider the same change from another angle, from the point of view of effort, of the trouble and responsibility involved in the two standpoints.

It is our contention, in complete contradiction to the usual view, that concentration upon reform and social use, as against the ideal of personal behaviour, is but one sign of the general tendency to avoid or postpone responsibility and effort. It is an attempt to do, in the moral sphere, what has been done in the material world, to find a short-cut effort-substitute. If in the everyday life, which to us is most important, it has been possible, and is thought praiseworthy, to avoid effort, and whenever, and so far as may be, to find a substitute for our own labour, why should not the same principle prevail in all other fields? It is our contention that it has prevailed, and that it was natural and logical that it should, when once the basis of life had been contracted.

It is our contention that the old-fashioned and despised

insistence on personal behaviour, which is but the basis of potential holiness, did exact a far higher degree of immediate effort, of need for immediate action, here and now.

In the earliest days of human civilization, we are told that Man adapted himself to his environment; he learned to do things, to differentiate himself from his fellows, according to the conditions in which he lived. Improvement in his implements followed this growth as a matter of course, and, in a sense, prepared for the machine, but the tool was still a tool; the bronze knife was more efficient than the flint, but it did not cut of itself. There was greater scope for human skill, not less, as implements improved, and a greater mastery over material things, but the emphasis was still on Man's adaptation to his environment; when a difficulty occurred in this ever-changing process of adaptation, it was a new challenge to his energy, but in the last centuries the emphasis has been shifting; it is now the environment that must be altered to suit the static nature of modern man.

Man's nature is accepted as supreme; man's will is paramount and must prevail, and this anthropocentric attitude to life has produced the amazing material achievements to which we are almost deadeningly accustomed. The whole energy and vitality of mankind has been expended upon environment, upon inanimate nature, to master and transform and utilize it to serve our ends, and, as a final phase, to save us trouble. It is as though the energy expended had been in fact transferred to the machine, it has obtained its power at our expense, and we, the creators, drained of energy, are carried, lifeless, in the turning wheels. As in the material, so in the moral, field, environment must be adapted to suit man; this is the typical view of the Reformer. Such and such a thing in life makes Man unhappy, therefore it must be removed; not, "Let us help him to face it bravely." When we are dealing with other people's troubles, with what makes them unhappy, it may be salutary that we should try to remedy, if we can, the external cause of their unhappiness, but if such a principle be once accepted, shall we not apply it also to ourselves?

When we are unhappy, we are usually conscious of definite external reasons for our unhappiness; if such and such obstacles were removed, we should be happy, and our natural reaction in this situation is to concentrate on removing the obstacles. We very seldom stop to consider whether something in ourselves may not be to blame for the effect which these same obstacles have upon us.

Supposing, for instance, we are afraid of something, some disaster, some disease perhaps—we are sure that we shall be quite happy so soon as the threat of that particular danger is over—but, are we? The doctor's diagnosis is favourable, our dividends pay once more, we consider ourselves safe and happy, but we are not really so, for the element in ourselves which was frightened is still the same, it is still there ready to respond to the next danger with the same fear; and other dangers will come, we may be sure: so long as we, in ourselves, are apprehensive, there will always be matter for our apprehension.

We shall find the same with all our other troubles, with envy and with greed and with ambition. It is only when, if ever, we turn our minds to the problem of our own nature and its weakness, when, if ever, we recognize the obstacle to our happiness in ourselves, that we shall be free from our unhappiness.

This is no new confusion. In the fourth century St. Augustine was confronted with the same tendency:

"'Bad times, troublous times,' thus men are saying. 'Let our lives be good and our times will be good. We make our times what we are!' "[1]

It is not only in the case of happiness; very often the difficulties that we encounter seem to prevent our spiritual wellbeing; we could be good, we are convinced we could, if only our circumstances could be different; yet the same holds good with even greater force when we are dealing with purely moral values. The impulse to escape is plausible. It is so important that we should be good, we should have all the help towards our good intentions, we ought not to subject them to too great a strain.

In each case the wish is to postpone the issue, to remove the conflict from our immediate power, to project the responsibility on to outward causes, to avoid an effort that is "here and now."

In opposition to this modern view, we have the teaching of a modern Saint:

> "*Il ne faut jamais, quand nous commettons une faute, l'attribuer à une cause physique, comme la maladie, ou le temps, mais convenir que cette chûte est due à notre imperfection, sans jamais nous décourager.*"[2]

Looking at it like this, we can see that the religious view which concentrates on personal sanctity is in fact recalling us to reality. It is the natural man who is seeking refuge in illusion, in an ideal fantasy existence where he and everybody will be good and happy, if only—something happens, that cannot happen.

The insistence on personal sanctity cuts across his fantasy with the unsympathetic douche of common sense.

"It is no good waiting for impossible conditions; you can

[1] St. Augustine, *Serm.* cccxi, VIII. 8.
[2] Ste. *Thérèse of Lisieux to her novices.*

be as happy and as good as you will ever be, both here and now, here in the midst of your uncongenial family with your colds and your chilblains and your toothaches, in the house you don't like, in the town you don't like, in the job you don't like."

This may be a hard saying, it may be repellent; to most of us it is, but it certainly is not "escapism."

We see a good illustration of this point in the case of a child when he first learns to walk. When he first tries to walk, he walks badly, he often stumbles and knocks himself and gets hurt. Any one who has watched such a child's progress, knows that his first impulse, when this happens, is anger with what he falls against. He smacks the floor on which he bumped his forehead:

"Naughty floor, to hurt poor Tommy, naughty, naughty chair to make poor Tommy fall!"

The old-fashioned nurse often encouraged this, on the ground that it distracted Tommy's attention from his pain if he was angry with the floor or chair, but the newer education appears in this case better, when it condemns such a method as retrograde. Tommy will only effectively avoid the pain of repeated tumbles by better walking, by more efficient control of his own little legs and feet, he will only learn how to control them better by realizing that what he does now is incomplete.

When you tell him the chair is to blame or the floor or the footstool, you postpone by so much more his real progress, you prepare for him just so many more tumbles, so much greater trouble when he learns the truth.

In Tommy's case the harm is temporary, for he will learn the truth in time, in spite of his nurse; he will probably learn by his own experience, by the joy of mastering his movements properly, by avoiding the chair or the stool, through his own skill: "I would have fallen then," he thinks, "if I had not been so clever—when I was a little boy, I would have fallen! The chair is the same chair, only I am different!"

That is the beginning of a true self-knowledge: if Tommy could go forward from this point, how happy and how good he might become—but all around him, and from every angle, public opinion will conspire against him.

It is not the chair now, that could not deceive him, but it is world-economics, or physical health. When he loses his temper and feels ashamed about it, he is told it was not his fault, he could not help it, his ductless glands had made him irritable: "Naughty ductless glands to provoke poor Tommy!"

Tommy would like to have controlled his temper, as earlier he has learned to control his legs, but the pressure gets too great as he grows older, the pressure of a machine-mastered world to make him, too, a cog in the machine. He cannot suppose the whole world mistaken, things cannot be in his power after all, it is no good his making any effort.

The fallacy in the Reformer's attitude is at bottom the same as the aristocratic Pagan's of whom he is indeed another aspect; he too builds his whole system on illusion, the illusion that what he rejects does not exist. As Aristocrat, he refused to accept the proletariat; as Reformer, he refuses to accept pain and evil; he assumes that human life should be made painless and easy, that it should be possible to abolish sorrow and failure and ill health and disappointment, all could be remedied by right arrangement; there is no need to develop courage or other adaptation to misfortune if all misfortune is removable. It is the old dogma of the Enlightenment, the perfectibility of man as man. If he cannot abolish death, he denies judgment, and the whole ultimate value that it implies; in this, as in everything, he is moderate. We might describe him from another angle as opting deliberately for Limbo, in preference to either Heaven or Hell.

He is like a man living inside a closed room where everything is perfectly arranged on a small scale of limited perfection. There is order and harmony and beauty in that room so long as its doors and windows are kept shuttered and nothing breaks in from the outer air. Its proportion and harmony are self-contained, dependent upon absolute isolation; its temperature is maintained by thermostat at level medium between cold and heat.

We must suppose this small closed room is built on the highest peak of some great mountain range; outside are the expanse of sky, of sun and moon and stars and cloud and wind, and the expanse below of all the earth, forests and fields and oceans and great cities, earthquakes and pestilence and war and sin—all are shut out, denied, repudiated, inside that tiny, perfect, closed-in room.

If it were possible to keep at bay the vast world outside indefinitely, the Pagan's way of life might have endured, but it is not. He may shut out the sky and sun and stars, but storm and earthquake will break in his doors; besides this, there are traitors in his midst. In every generation there are some who will not stay imprisoned in that room; who will, in spite of all his prohibitions, open the shutters and look out and see, open the windows and breathe the outer air; he cannot, in fact, keep his isolation.

This simile will seem a paradox; it has been for so long taken for granted that the Rationalist, the Good Pagan, has opened to us a far wider world than the poor Christian could enjoy, that whatever weakness be found in his position, freedom and breadth of vision must be his. This view is based on a misconception, on a misleading scale of values, it assumes the mechanical quantity dimension in which alone our horizon has been enlarged, but we do not and cannot live in such a medium only, even the proletarian has a soul.

The believing Christian of the Middle Ages knew less than we know about astronomic space, the physical world was limited for him, but he belonged also to another order, enfranchized to it through his baptism. In body he was imprisoned, it may be, in a far smaller world than we know now, and limited by lack of telescopes, but in soul he partook of a much larger freedom, he could transcend the bonds of time and space; for him an expanding universe was unessential.

Eternity and infinity to-day have for most of us a mathematical significance, if indeed they do mean anything at all, but to the Christian of the Age of Faith they were the charter of his liberty; he shared in the infinite and the eternal, his life was partly lived in such dimensions.

This relation of the individual soul to infinity is something quite incomprehensible to the modern Pagan; it is the most difficult idea to translate into Pagan terms.

This is one of the most striking points of difference between the old philosophic Pagan and the modern. The ancient philosopher had to a great extent the totalitarian hierarchic point of view; he saw the individual soul in relation to the Kosmos, himself in relation to the Divine Order, but in this, as in so much else, his ideas have disintegrated;[1] the hierarchic conception has been superseded by the atomic.

The typical modern is essentially atomic, there is little

---

[1] Cf., Plato, *Laws* x, 903[B].

"The Power who cares for the Universe has disposed all things with a view to the preservation and excellence of the whole system in which each part according to the measure of its capacity does and suffers what properly belongs to it."

continuity, little connection in the different forms and facets of life as he sees it passing. It is to him like a series of moving pictures, disjointed fleeting impressions, moods, emotions; we see this state of mind reflected very clearly in much current literature and art; James Joyce and T. S. Eliot are examples, and much obscure contemporary free verse, the surrealists and their like in painting; the cinema is its more popular expression. There is at times a positive rejection of the whole notion of a reasoned form, an almost frantic negation of any order or meaning pervading the seemingly accidental chaos.

We can see the same tendency in more personal issues, the repugnance from taking long horizons, from looking ahead, planning life with a purpose. The individual becomes even to himself non-continuous, he is only what he is at the passing moment; what he was or will be is dissociated in his own mind, almost intentionally, from the present. This has one immediate practical advantage, he is absolved from all responsibility for his actions; what he did last week cannot affect him, he is unconnected with his last week's self.

The extreme difference of outlook which must follow from this contrast between the atomic and totalitarian states of mind, can hardly be exaggerated or overstated; it pervades and influences all our actions and leads to the most complete misunderstanding. To the Pagan mind of this atomic type any emphasis on individual value as such is repugnant. He thinks of the individual as an atom, cut off and separate and unrelated; he thinks of individual perfection as in opposition to the common good. Concentration on personal sanctity is to him essentially self-centred and egotistic, because to him the self is isolated, one separate and competing human atom. The whole conception of a Divine Order, a unity and wholeness which can be shared, the idea expressed in a Communion of

Saints, a Living Church, a Mystical Body, has, and can have, no sense whatever to the atomic mind. It is the same with eternity and infinity; these are essentially totalitarian concepts, hard enough for any limited human mind to grasp, quite unintelligible to the atomic modern. To such a mind the whole idea of eternal value is constricted into material, temporal terms. If we say that an action has eternal consequences, he transposes it into a concrete time dimension:

> "You'll have pie,
> In the sky,
> By and by,
> ... It's a lie!"

is an illustration of this transposition.

To insist that the action has eternal value, here and now, is to him nonsense, a contradiction in terms of the most flagrant kind. This explains also the usual assumption that belief in immortality detracts from the interest and importance of this life. In one sense this is true; the believer will, in so far as his belief is strong and effective, be less at the mercy of vicissitude, he will be less desolated in disaster, perhaps less exhilarated by good fortune. The imperturbability and serenity of martyrs is of course extremely rare, but a far milder form of such detachment does in fact often strike the attention of the Pagan as unpleasantly characteristic of the Christian. To take an extreme and obvious example, death is less final and less terrifying to the believer in Eternal Life, and, in the degree to which his faith is real, this difference in his attitude to death is noticeable in his ordinary life. The same is true of pain or suffering; he may and should feel pity and compassion, but he does not experience the same indignation, the same outraged and rebellious anger in face of suffering, in himself—or in others—that the Pagan feels, and the Good

Pagan who attaches great importance to humanitarian sensibility is at times genuinely shocked and scandalized by what he considers lack of proper feeling. He feels the Christian attitude inhuman, and that, to him, is extreme condemnation.

We admit that the Christian is, in a sense, detached from life, that his response to human joy and fear is less whole-hearted than the immediate reaction of the Pagan; his treasure is not here, he admits it, he is a citizen of a Heavenly City, and yet we still maintain, in contradiction, that, the more he is living in the Heavenly City, the more will his life be, here and now, enriched. Here, as so often in the Christian stand-point, we seem to be faced with a contradiction, a truth that must be expressed in paradox.

> "They alone are able truly to enjoy this world, who begin with the world unseen. They alone enjoy it, who have abstained from it. . . . They alone inherit it, who take it as a shadow of the world to come, who, for that world to come, relinquish it."[1]

From the atomic point of view, each act of will, each personal decision, is separate and ephemeral, no inevitable consequences are involved, nor are accepted; our actions are without meaning, insignificant, except in so far as they achieve results of some importance in the material world.

Only a small minority of people have any opportunity for such action; the enormous majority of men and women live out their lives in trivial circumstances in which there is no opportunity for action of importance in this world. What does it matter how they use their will in the small field in which they move and live, it will make so little difference to the world, or to themselves, or to anyone at all, why should they bother to exert themselves? This attitude makes life uninteresting.

[1] Newman. *Parochial and Plain Sermons*, vi, 93.

For the Christian, in contrast to this dullness, there is constant daily necessity for action. His will can be related to God's Will, his suffering to the suffering of Christ; each day is thus, to him, of moment, each day he has his act of will to make; here and now, in this world, in the conditions of his material life, he lives in terms of the eternal value.

If we are living our life, here and now, in relation to the supernatural life, each act and aspect of our natural life is lived at the same time in another medium, in what we have called before the X Dimension, and in the degree to which this X Dimension is infinite and eternal and supernatural, the trivial acts of our quite human life partake of this X quality as well, they are transformed, they change their character. No act, no decision, no exercise of will, is, in relation to God, of no importance. It is of no consequence at all that, materially, our acts affect nobody, that no effect is produced in our environment by what we do; if we are operating in this X Dimension, everything is of value, everything matters. The Christian always is "about his Father's business."

We might compare this life to an unlit Chinese lantern with patterns of dark and light in different colours; we see the patterns, but they are without meaning to us, undifferentiated, of no interest, and then we light the candle inside the lantern; the lantern is the same, the patterns upon it are the same as they were, but now, in the light shining through them from within, the same shapes and colours have been transformed, we see the beauty and value of the pattern, each line, each patch of colour has a reason.

So does the knowledge of supernatural value, underlying and permeating the natural world, illumine and explain our actual life.

Insistence on this truth is to be found in almost all religious

exposition; perhaps it is best expressed by Francis Thompson
in his poem:

> "O world invisible, we view thee,
>   O world intangible, we touch thee.
>   O world unknowable, we know thee.
>   Inapprehensible, we clutch thee!"

Yet even that, explicit as it would seem, can be misunderstood; Mr. Lionel Curtis, in the book already referred to, has
quoted that same poem to illumine his thesis that the Kingdom
of Heaven is the British Commonwealth!

Once more we have taken the war into our enemy's camp,
and turned back on him the accusation made against us.

In direct contradiction to the usual view, we maintain that
the effect of Pagan concentration on this world has been to
drain present life of all its value. We would say that human
life deprived of God is like a human body deprived of life.
The same limbs are there, the same features, the same form,
but all that gave it meaning has gone from it, and we know
that the body itself cannot last when the life has left it.

We would say that the Good Pagan is like the jealous lover
who has killed his beloved to keep her all his own. He holds
her body cold and inanimate, he is the master of the lifeless
thing, but all that made her what she was, is gone. He holds
an empty likeness in his arms and soon even that will perish
and putrefy.

VIII

We have now considered our Contracting Universe in
various aspects as it affects our lives, our points of view, in
apparently different and unconnected ways, and we have tried
to trace the different changes, which we agree are taking place

around us, back to one common source, revolt from God. We
have tried to examine the process, if it is indeed one process,
from differing points of view, but always, so far, we seem to
have been taking the standpoint of the ousted governing
class.

We have, as was inevitable, taken the Christian view in the
dispute, we have explained what to us seems to be happening,
on the assumption of the Christian standpoint, but we have
found that, on some points, we and the Good Pagan are in
agreement; in face of a common enemy we know, we are drawn
closer to our partial friends; in face of the present automatic
materialism, the barbarization of life that is before us, Christian
and Good Pagan feel common cause, yet the difference between
them is there and is not bridged, and nowhere is it deeper or
more pronounced than in our relation to the Proletarian
himself.

This may seem at first another paradox, it is in fact more of
a platitude.

Let us now try and see the whole process we have examined,
so far as we can, through proletarian eyes.

We have described the existing situation as a gradual
domination of society from below, through all the different
phases of social life; the poor man, the stupid man, the idle
man, the failure is less at a disadvantage than formerly. We
have seen that increasing dependence on the machine has
equalized, and is equalizing more, the natural inequalities of
mankind. We have seen that this process of equalization, in
the form in which it has come, is increasingly hampering and
penalizing merit, increasingly compensating those without it.
This process gives greater influence to precisely those elements
in society which by their nature were least influential, the
undifferentiated, non-excelling masses.

Now, in as much as the undistinguished are numerically far superior, it is right that, on any democratic basis, their welfare should be the decisive consideration. Even without a democratic bias, on principles of any social justice, the welfare of the majority of our fellows should be our first concern. If it were possible to maintain convincingly that the proletarianization of society, the domination of the higher and more individual mind by the lower and less developed, was in fact conducive to the common good, that the greatest happiness of the greatest number was in truth promoted thus, it would be incumbent on us to accept a process which was to us personally distasteful, or even fatal.

In trying to look at any question fairly, we must first detach it from personal interests, we must be prepared to find justice in a conclusion which to us or our own kind is detrimental.

In the language of the Good Pagan, we may state it:

"It is not necessarily for the common good that I, or such as I, should prosper at the expense of others than myself."

In the language of the Christian it is simply:

"What I like may not prove to be God's Will."

Without this knowledge and acceptance of it, no just consideration is possible of any question that affects ourselves; with it ever present to us, we may endeavour to discuss the welfare of the majority.

This brings us face to face with a new question: in what does human welfare consist? by what criterion do we mean to judge it?

We are back at our fundamental difference, the meaning we attach to the term "good."

It is probably true that at no time in history have material advantages been so widely distributed, when both education and entertainment are so easy of access to everybody, when so much thought and money has been expended on what are called the social services. The ordinary population of civilized countries is better off materially than it has ever been, yet these things are in themselves only means to the desired end of human welfare, and we are back again at our first question: what do we mean by it? how can we judge it? The Pagan would define it as happiness. The greatest happiness of the greatest number is the simplest and most comprehensive expression of this judgment. If we apply this standard to our question, we shall ask whether more people are more happy now, in the proletarian epoch, than they were before, or would be otherwise. If we put our question thus, the answer is, surely, no; it is probable that more people are more unhappy now than they ever were.

The relation of happiness to material welfare is difficult to assess with certainty; it is obvious that physical privation and discomfort do ordinarily tend to unhappiness, but the attempt to identify the two is surely, quite as obviously, untrue.

The interior quality of true happiness has been emphasized by all serious schools of thought from the earliest philosophers to the present day, the Good Pagan has been as insistent as the Christian; yet, as with other transcendental value-judgments, this assertion has never been generally acted upon. We do all in our daily lives assume dependence on external circumstances, but are we not perpetually disillusioned? Are we not constantly finding for ourselves that some desired change in our condition leaves us, as before, unsatisfied?

If we are born into the governing class, into positions of privilege and comfort, most of our personal experience will be among the equally privileged; among such people to-day in England, physical want is practically unknown; no child in such circles will be undernourished, no family will be cold for lack of coal, yet how many of our friends do we count happy? I doubt if the proportion is any larger than it would be among the working class.

Happiness is too vague a definition, it does not tell us what we want to know.

Why are human beings not in practice happy when they have enough to eat and warm clothes to wear, when they have opportunities for enjoyment their fathers never dreamed of?

It is easy to make general explanations, such as insecurity, dread of unemployment or of war, but we do not find such explanations valid. It is true, as we have already noticed, that there is a widespread sense of insecurity among all classes in society, we have even given this as an example of proletarianization, but we maintain it to be more subjective, more the result of our own state of mind than the result of outer circumstances.

It is true that there is fear of unemployment, more especially in certain areas, but to counterbalance that we must remember that there has always been such fear, and the social services to which we have referred do greatly mitigate its penalties.

Although a larger proportion of people lack employment, the actual lack of employment, when it comes, is infinitely less painful and desperate than it once was.

The fear of war is also a real fear, lurking uncomfortably in the background, but the number of people consciously affected by any active fear of war is small. We have seen already, in considering the reformer, that the whole tendency of the modern world lies in emphasis upon external factors, the desire to externalize our difficulties; if we are in our selves insecure, we shall seize anxiously on outward reasons to justify our insecurity, there will be always in our circumstances something or other upon which to fix.

If we continue our inquiry further into the reason for

unhappiness, we shall find it most often in personal relations; someone has been unkind, someone is difficult, we are married to the wrong person, our friends have misunderstood us, or, in the public field, our employers are unjust, or our political opponents behave badly, some wrong adjustment between human beings, again it is an interior difficulty, on one side or the other, perhaps both; there is need for a change of heart, for personal effort to be what we are not, to become better, but the whole mental atmosphere of our time is unfavourable to such a direct solution.

In all these causes of unhappiness we have seen unhappiness to be dependent on some interior personal element, in our selves and in the selves of other people, far more than on material circumstances.

The Good Pagan would have said:

"Know thyself."

The Christian says:

"The Kingdom of Heaven is within you."

But we pay little attention to either of them.

IX

We have seen that both Good Pagan and Christian are agreed that happiness is not dependent on outer things, yet we admit that to most ordinary people the degree of self-mastery and detachment advocated appears too difficult to be worth attempting. Can we not find some less exalted and less esoteric standard by which to measure human happiness?

I think some standard of the sort is found in the sense of satisfaction that we feel in doing well something that we have to do, in fulfilling some function which we recognize as ours. The happiness of a mother with her child, if analysed, is largely of this nature, it is not only, nor even principally, the individual love between two persons, it is the sense of doing what she is meant for, of fulfilling her function in the scheme of things. In so artificial a society as ours, the simple and natural functional relations are largely interfered with and disturbed, but in the satisfaction of achieving any task assigned us, we find the same sense of fulfilling a purpose, of doing something we were meant to do. Some form of activity seems necessary, although activity may at times be passive, very few people can be happy idle.

When a man has work to do that he does badly, which is unsuited to his capacity or temperament, he will dislike the work and will resent it, but he will not be happy doing nothing.

We must agree that, in some form or other, we do all want to do what we do best, to feel that there is some use and value in what we do, that we are functioning as we were meant to function.

It is precisely this quality of personal usefulness that is so lacking in a machine civilization, you cannot achieve the personal satisfaction of doing what you *can* do, with a machine; you as an individual are not wanted, what you do is as well done by someone else, or by a cog-wheel; you are not needed; there is no place for you, no fundamental relation between you and others, no dependence of the parts upon the whole in the atomic, equalitarian world.

This sense of having no place, of not being needed, is acutely felt among the unemployed; to them it may seem only social maladjustment, to be remedied by planned industry, but we suggest that the unwanted unemployed are but a more extreme example of a whole world of maladjusted workers.

The sense of not being wanted, never having had a chance, of wasted potentialities, of frustration, is one of the commonest forms of unhappiness in the modern world; we suggest that it is a direct result of a falsely based equalitarian order.

It is not true that everyone is equal either in physical or in intellectual powers; it is not true that everyone is equally fitted to govern the country, to make laws or to enforce them, to teach or to be taught; not everyone can appreciate music or mathematics, or dictate the standards of art and literature; and assertions of such non-existent equality are harmful. In a society based on such a false foundation we have an overwhelming number of people who are trying to do what is unsuited to them, who are trying to be what they were not meant to be, and when they discover, as they are bound to, that in this chaotic world they are misfits, they have no refuge and no consolation; there is no place for them, and that is all.

It is inherent in the religious outlook that there is a "right use" for everything, still more is there a right use for every person, and this implies the hierarchic order in which each kind of person has his place. According to this standpoint, being happy is always and only doing what you are meant to do, doing God's Will, whatever that may be.

According to this standpoint, God's Will may be done as completely in doing nothing, or in doing trivial things, provided they are done with right intention, as in some world-shattering achievement; in the X Dimension, the supernatural medium of existence, it is within the reach of everybody to do what they are meant to do, completely, to fulfil to the utmost the potentiality of their nature, which is the doing of God's Will for them.

"God has created me to do Him some definite service, He has committed some work to me, which He has not

committed to another, I have my mission. I may never
know it in this life, but I shall be told it in the next. I
have a part in a great work; I am a link in a chain, a
bond of connection between persons. He has not created
me for naught. I shall do good. I shall do His work."[1]

From another and quite different source we have the same
truth expressed by Milton in the famous sonnet on his blindness:

> "His state
> Is kingly, thousands at His bidding speed,
> And post o'er land and ocean without rest;
> They also serve, who only stand and wait."

We have already compared the hierarchic order to an
orchestra in which each humblest player has his part, necessary
but dependent on the others. We have considered the confusion which results from an equalitarian revolt among the
players and the attempt to play with no conductor. In the
present connection we might carry our illustration one stage
further, and imagine the state of our orchestra if, in addition
to the equalitarian revolt, we were faced with players to whom
music of any kind was unintelligible, who could not distinguish
one note from another and denied the existence of laws of
harmony.

We are faced to-day with such a situation in regard to Divine
laws and the supernatural life. The stage is there, and the
instruments and the players, but they are all stone deaf, and do
not even know it; how are we to produce our symphony?

In this, as in so much else, there seems to be a complete
reversal of what ought to be. It is admitted generally, to-day,
that certain people have a religious sense; it is to be respected
and recognized, there is no wish to coerce them or repress
them, but it is regarded as peculiar, like having second sight

[1] Newman. *Meditations and Devotions*, 400–1.

or being double jointed, it is assumed that most people have not got it.

On the other hand, we find it taken for granted that everyone is capable of artistic appreciation, of intellectual judgment and education; these are for all, religion for the few. It is difficult to understand a judgment so patently at variance with the facts.

It might be argued that the inspired artist or the creative intellectual could find in his æsthetic or mental life a kind of spiritual substitute; he has at least in his own world of thought a window from the prison of here and now, but in the case of the poor simple man such substitutes become a mockery; they are not for such men, as he knows himself to be.

It is only in the history of religion that we find no difference of caste or intellect, no barriers to any type of mind. Great saints have been great intellectuals; they have, as often, been illiterate. They have been artistic, cultured, noble; they have, equally, been rustic, crude and without taste. The language of holiness is the only one that needs no dictionary, no translation, yet in this bewildering age of ours it is judged unsuited to the multitude.

There was a story told by one of the early liberal labour leaders which bears on this.

A party of visitors was being shown over a coal mine. It was an old coal mine, where conditions were very bad; the passage down which they went grew lower and lower; it was hot and wet and most uncomfortable. They approached a coal face where a miner was obliged to work all day in a crouched position, unable to sit upright. The visitors were full of indignation at the intolerable conditions of such work.

As they approached down the long dark passage, they could hear the man's voice, singing at his work:

"Were the whole realm of nature mine,
That were an offering far too small;
Love so amazing, so divine,
Demands my soul, my life, my all!"[1]

and the visitors were silenced.

The miner of to-day works under better conditions; he has shorter hours, higher wages, and pit-head baths, but the "Love so amazing, so divine" has been taken from him, or rather it has been denied him and hidden from him. No pit-head baths can compensate him for it.

If we consider, for a moment, what is involved in this substitution, we have before us a complete example of what we may call the Pagan revaluation; we may see it here in both its strength and its weakness. The rationalist, confronted with the miner who is wrapt in contemplation of the Cross, feels a compassion for him that is twofold. He pities him for the hardness of his life, his dangerous and disagreeable work, his poverty, his servitude; he also pities him, and perhaps even more, because he is living in a fantasy. He is, according to the rationalist, like a man drugged with opium, or with drink;[2] he is blinding himself to his own misery by dependence on a dream compensation. Because he has found the world so hard and cold, he has invented an all-loving Saviour, to whom he, in his impotence, is dear; he projects upon this imaginary Saviour all the love and gratitude for which he has found no recipient in this world. The bitter truth has been too hard for him, but in the opinion of the rationalist it is his duty to recall him to it.

So long as he can escape in fantasy, he will not trouble

[1] *Hymns Ancient & Modern*, 108.
[2] Cf., Lenin, *Socialism and Religion*.
    "Religion is a kind of spiritual intoxicant, in which the slaves of capital drown their humanity and blunt their desire for a decent human existence."

about real things; he will not concentrate on actual evils, which can and must be altered or abolished.

The miner with his supernatural Saviour is, to the rationalist, a deluded traveller, lured from the sure road of material progress by phantom visions of the Will o' the Wisp; he does not consider, even for a moment, the possibility of his own view being mistaken, the possibility that it may be the miner who has seen the actual truth and understood it, a truth that he himself, with all his learning, may have somehow failed to understand or see.

The reforms, the whole position, of the Pagan presuppose the material nature of the human beast; they assume that purely animal well-being can, in the end, completely satisfy him; it is our contention that the whole development of our civilization disproves that theory.

We would say that in his equalitarianism he has degraded the whole human race, in his apparent championship of the outcast he has insulted and has injured him, for he, as much as the most civilized, has, and in essence is, an immortal soul. We would say that the simple man has been exploited, most cruelly and completely, by the Pagan who professed to labour for his benefit, and now he is awaking to his condition. He has been aroused and armed but not instructed, and we are at the mercy of his revenge.

X

If it were not for this extreme delusion, we might wonder at the light-hearted, almost frivolous way in which the best of Pagans is prepared to shut out his supernatural life from the poor man; we might say that he has committed spiritual murder, but we can see it now more nearly as manslaughter. He does not mean to murder anybody, he does not even see what he has killed.

In most fields of human knowledge or experience we hesitate to express a strong opinion if we ourselves are ignorant of the subject; we should not enter the lists against Einstein if we ourselves had no knowledge of mathematics, we should be reluctant to condemn Beethoven if we ourselves could not tell two tunes apart, yet in the field of spiritual knowledge it seems to be accounted reasonable for those who have neither experience nor knowledge, who have never tried to understand the subject, to offer the most dogmatic criticism.

The ignorance of the elements of religion is astounding among enlightened intellectual Pagans who believe themselves to know what can be known. They have never heard the names of the great Saints, or bothered to read spiritual writers.

Educated men and women who would not dream of judging literature by the *feuilletons* of a Sunday newspaper, or art from the bargain basement souvenir, are ready and willing to accept for religion its lowest and most sensational travesty.

When some fantastic revivalist is exposed from time to time as fraudulent, such critics have disposed of revelation.

In fairness to the Pagan iconoclast, we must realize his abysmal ignorance. When he takes from the miner, so lightheartedly, the amazing and divine Love by which he lived, he has not the least notion what it is, in truth, that he is destroying.

We may liken him to an innocent boisterous child who knocks a priceless vase from the chimney-piece, remarking that it took up too much room, he must have more space on which to stand his toys. If you explain to the child that this white vase, which seemed to him so plain and common and ugly, was in fact an irreplaceable Chinese porcelain, preserved through possibly three thousand years, he will as a rule express some slight regret; if he had known, he would have been more careful, he would have only pushed it on one side, he would perhaps have even looked at it!

We have most of us, at some time or other, known human love; we have most of us felt at some time for some person a devotion which has transformed life for us, which has transfused and enriched the texture of our everyday lives; with the object of this love beside us, the dingiest surroundings became delightful, the dreariest occupation interesting. It may have happened that this did not last, that there was some illusion in our love, but very few good people would have gladly and deliberately destroyed it, yet we find that the average Good Pagan has no compunction in destroying, where he can, the Love of God. In the case of a human devotion that is misplaced, it is sometimes possible for a disinterested onlooker to see quite clearly, and perhaps with pity, the element of illusion that exists. He too may see the beloved and speak with her; he may see that she is not really beautiful nor conspicuous for any of the virtues with which our infatuation has endowed her. The onlooker is in this case at no disadvantage compared with the deluded devotee, but when we are dealing with the Love of God, the position is immeasurably altered. The Pagan and the Christian cannot compare their so contrasted valuations of God, because only one has any knowledge of Him.

The Pagan is in no position to judge that Love of God is waste of time, or exaggerated, or unwarranted by circumstances, unless he too knows God and does not love Him; and such a situation seems unknown.

It would appear, from most religious writers, that there is a

great variation of degree in what we call the knowledge and
love of God, but there is universal agreement that the two go
together in intensity:

> "For as we know Him, so do we love Him. If we
> know Him but little, we shall love Him but little."[1]

To know and to love would seem inseparable. Against this
wealth of direct testimony we have no direct oppositional
view at all. All that the disbeliever can say in answer, is:

"I do not see it. You say there is something there, I say
there is not."

In such a case there are two possible explanations. Two
people are looking, one sees and one does not. It is possible
that the one seeing is deluded; it is equally possible that the
other is blind.

From the believer's point of view, what he sees can be seen
by everybody, the Star that he follows is for all mankind: "A
light to lighten the Gentiles and those that are sitting in the
valley of the shadow of death." It is in no sense reserved for
him alone. But we may ask what proportion of unbelievers
have wanted to see the Star, have looked for it? I think that
if they were to answer truly, we should find that hardly any of
them had bothered.

Can we not train our eyes, our ears, our understanding, to
discern and appreciate forms of sensible beauty, to which,
uncaring, we were blind and deaf, which, without effort, we
could not understand? May it not be so with spiritual
apprehension?

> "He that hath eyes to see, let him see;
> he that hath ears to hear, let him understand!"

Even then, not all had either eyes nor ears.

[1] Blessed Angela of Foligno.

XI

We have ascribed the failure of the Good Pagan civilization, through all its varying and degenerating phases, to the one primal fault from which it sprang, the denial of God and all that went with God, the rejection of the Supernatural Order in all its bearings, inner and outer, both in the human soul and in the world.

We have traced it through its different forms and phases, its failure to deal with actual human nature, to recognize sin and pain and loss and the needs of an immortal soul; we have seen it as a gigantic effort of idolatry and rebellion, an attempt to replace the Divine by the Human, the Supernatural by the Natural, the Spiritual by the Material, the Eternal by the Temporal, an effort to compress our whole existence into a moderate and twilight Limbo—a passionate limitation of all life.

We have seen that this gigantic attempt is failing, that by excluding Heaven we have not abolished Hell, that by denying redemption we have not been redeemed, the sinner is still there, in the world and in ourselves.

"Unhappy man that I am," he is still crying, "who shall deliver me from the body of this death?"

The Good Pagan has not delivered him and he cannot, he has told him that no deliverance is needed, that it will all come right, he need not worry. But he does worry, and will always worry, because, though he may not know it, he has a soul; because his soul was made by God for Himself, and cannot rest until it rests in Him.

We cannot divide ourselves from the sinner and outcast; he is with us, he is a part of us, and of the Pagan too.

Even the Good Pagan is unhappy, because, in his own despite, he too wants God.

> "For this is the cause why we be not all in ease of heart and soul, that we seek here rest in these things that be so little, and know not our God, that is Almighty, All-wise, All-good."[1]

This is the one answer to all our questions, the only solution to our difficulties. It is as true to-day as it was in the fourteenth century when Julian lived, or in the fourth century for St. Augustine. We have not outgrown it, and we shall not outgrow it; it is applicable to the modern mind as truly as it was to the first Christians.

[1] Julian of Norwich. *Revelations of Divine Love*, V.

Date Due

N 9 - '48	JAN 2 3 '59	
N 2 3 '48	FEB 1 0 '60	
N 7 - '48	MAY 2 1 '60	
N 3 '48	NOV 7 '61	
JAN 2 9 '50	NOV 2 9 '81	
F 15 '50	AP 5 '93	
AUG 1 '50		
FEB 2 - '51		
MAR 2 0 '54		
JAN 1 7 '55		
FEB 1 5 '55		
MAR 2 '55		
FEB 4 0 '56		
MAY 1 '56		
NOV 9 '56		
OCT 2 6 '56		
NOV 3 '56		
NOV 1 6 '56		
DEC 2 - '56		

CPSIA information can be obtained
at www.ICGtesting.com
Printed in the USA
BVHW050316070223
658034BV00003B/56

9 781014 103826